Kevin O. Samson

HYPER LIGHT BREAKER GAME GUIDE

From Combat Basics to Expert-Level Tactics, Everything You Need to Overcome the Abyss King and Dominate Every Boss Fight and Encounter

**Copyright © 2024 by Kevin O. Samson
All rights reserved.**

No part of this publication may be reproduced, distributed, or transmitted in any form or by any means, including photocopying, recording, or other electronic or mechanical methods, without the prior written permission of the publisher, except in the case of brief quotations embodied in critical reviews and certain other non-commercial uses permitted by copyright law. For permission requests, write to the publisher at the address below

Disclaimer

The information provided in this book is based on the author's personal experience and research of *Hyper Light Breaker* as of its latest available version. While every effort has been made to ensure the accuracy and completeness of the content, the author and publisher make no guarantees regarding the game's future updates, patches, or changes that may alter the game mechanics, strategies, or content discussed in this book.

No Affiliation with the Developers or Publishers

This book is an independent guide and is not affiliated, endorsed, or authorized by Heart Machine, Arc Games, or any other official developers or publishers of *Hyper Light Breaker*. All trademarks, service marks, and game-related terms mentioned in this book are the property of their respective owners.

Use of This Guide

The strategies, tips, and content provided in this book are intended for entertainment and informational purposes only. By using this guide, you agree that the author and publisher are not responsible for any consequences, including but not limited to, game performance issues, damages, or other unintended outcomes.

Fair Use

This book includes references to *Hyper Light Breaker*, which is copyrighted by Heart Machine and Arc Games. The use of these references is in accordance with fair use for educational, commentary, and review purposes. The inclusion of such content does not imply any ownership or authorship of the game or any of its elements.

Updates and Changes

Since video games often receive updates that can change gameplay mechanics, content, and other aspects, the information in this book may become outdated over time. The author and publisher are not responsible for any discrepancies between the content of this book and the game's latest version. Please check for updates and community resources to stay current with new features or adjustments.

By purchasing and reading this book, you acknowledge that you understand the terms of this disclaimer.

Table of contents

DISCLAIMER 3
INTRODUCTION 8
CHAPTER 1 13
   GETTING STARTED WITH HYPER LIGHT BREAKER 13
      Overview of the Game and World 13
      First Steps: Basic Controls and Gameplay Mechanics 15
      Core Gameplay Mechanics 18
      Choosing Your Breaker: Classes, Abilities, and Playstyles 19
CHAPTER 2 22
   UNDERSTANDING THE WORLD OF HYPER LIGHT BREAKER 22
      The Overgrowth: Exploring the Vast World 22
      The Biomes: Diversity in Environment and Challenge 23
      Environmental Storytelling: A World with History 25
      Movement Mechanics: Hoverboards, Gliders, and Wall Climbing
      26
      Wall Climbing: Overcoming Verticality 28
CHAPTER 3 31
   COMBAT AND WEAPONS IN HYPER LIGHT BREAKER 31
      Mastering Melee and Ranged Combat 31
      Melee Combat: Close Quarters, Powerful Strikes 31
      Ranged Combat: Precision and Distance 34
      Best Weapon Combinations for Different Playstyles 36
      Combat Tips: How to Take Down Enemies Efficiently 38
      Managing Health, Energy, and Resources During Fights 40
CHAPTER 4 43
   THE ROLE OF ABILITIES AND CLASSES IN HYPER LIGHT BREAKER 43
      Breakdown of Breaker Classes 43
      Key Abilities and Their Impact on Gameplay 47
      How to Build and Customize Your Breaker for Success 50

CHAPTER 5 54

   BOSS BATTLES: DEFEAT THE REGIONAL BOSSES IN *HYPER LIGHT BREAKER*........54
      Preparing for Boss Fights: Essential Tips and Strategies 54
      Regional Boss Walkthroughs: How to Defeat Each Boss 57
      Special Tactics for Multiplayers in Boss Fights 61

CHAPTER 6 64

   THE ABYSS KING: YOUR FINAL CHALLENGE 64
      Preparing for the Final Showdown 64
      Abyss King Boss Fight Strategy 67
      General Boss Fight Tips 70

CHAPTER 7 72

   MULTIPLAYER MODE: TEAMWORK AND CO-OP STRATEGIES..........................72
      Setting Up Multiplayer: How to Play with Friends......................72
      Co-op Tips: Best Roles and Strategies for Teams........................74
      Working Together to Defeat the Abyss King 78

CHAPTER 8 81

   EXPLORING THE HUB CITY IN *HYPER LIGHT BREAKER*....................................81
      What You Can Do in the Hub Between Runs 81
      NPC Interactions: Understanding Comic Book Panels and Storytelling 85
      Shops, Upgrades, and Secrets to Unlock in the Hub 87

CHAPTER 9 90

   SECRETS, EASTER EGGS, AND UNLOCKABLES IN *HYPER LIGHT BREAKER*............90
      Hidden Features and Special Secrets 90
      How to Unlock Easter Eggs and Bonus Content 93
      Tips for Finding All the Collectibles 95

CHAPTER 10 98

   ADVANCED TIPS FOR MASTERING *HYPER LIGHT BREAKER* 98
      Advanced Combat Techniques and Tricks 98
      How to Optimize Abilities and Gear for Maximum Efficiency....102
      Managing Runs: Resource Gathering, Upgrades, and More 104

CHAPTER 11 107

TROUBLESHOOTING AND FREQUENTLY ASKED QUESTIONS 107
   Solving Common Issues in Hyper Light Breaker 107
   Frequently Asked Questions by New and Experienced Players .. 111
   Performance and Technical Tips for a Smooth Experience 113

Introduction

Welcome to *Hyper Light Breaker*

Welcome, Breaker! You've entered the world of *Hyper Light Breaker*, a thrilling and visually stunning roguelike adventure from the brilliant minds at Heart Machine, the creators of *Hyper Light Drifter*. As a successor to their beloved 2016 title, *Hyper Light Breaker* elevates the experience with a massive, open-world setting, strategic combat, and heart-pounding action.

In this guide, we'll dive into everything you need to conquer the Overgrowth and face the mighty Abyss King. Whether you're a first-time player or a seasoned veteran of the Hyper Light universe, this guide will be your ultimate companion. I'm here to provide expert tips, strategies, and insights to make sure you don't just survive—you thrive.

By the end of this guide, you'll have mastered the game's intricate combat systems, unlocked powerful abilities, and learned how to make the most of your random world runs. This isn't just a guide—it's a roadmap to becoming the most powerful Breaker the Overgrowth has ever seen.

What You'll Learn from This Guide

This guide isn't just about walking you through the basics—it's designed to make you a true *Hyper Light Breaker* expert. Here's a sneak peek of what you'll find:

- **The Essential Game Mechanics**: Learn the ins and outs of combat, movement, and exploration. We'll break down how to make the most of your abilities, weapons, and tools, whether you're playing solo or with friends.

- **Character Classes and Builds**: *Hyper Light Breaker* offers different Breaker classes, each with unique abilities. We'll guide you through the best builds for your playstyle, whether you like to rush in with sword blazing or play it safe with ranged combat.

- **Boss Strategies**: Facing down the regional bosses is no small feat. I'll walk you through each one, sharing strategies that work and breaking down their attack patterns so you can take them down efficiently.

- **The Abyss King Fight**: Every Breaker's ultimate challenge. We'll ensure you're prepared to face the Abyss King in all his terrifying glory, with tips that will guarantee your success in this epic showdown.

- **Multiplayer Tactics**: *Hyper Light Breaker* isn't just a solo experience. We'll provide you with co-op strategies to make sure your team is working together to take down the toughest enemies and bosses.

- **Exploring the Hub City and Secrets**: There's more to the game than just fighting—there are hidden secrets, upgrades, and an entire city to explore. I'll share where to find these and how to unlock all the hidden gems scattered throughout the game world.

In short, this guide will help you **master the game**, **explore every corner of the world**, and **defeat every enemy** that stands in your way. Get ready to break free from the limitations of death and randomness and start making each run count!

Tips for Making the Most of Your Gameplay Experience

Hyper Light Breaker is a game of exploration, experimentation, and, most importantly, **learning from failure**. Every time you die (and trust me, you will), the game will throw something new at you. And this is exactly where the fun lies. Here are a few expert tips to make your gameplay experience as smooth and rewarding as possible:

1. **Embrace the Randomness**: This is a roguelike, which means each death is a chance to learn and improve. Don't get frustrated when the world changes; instead, view it as a new opportunity to explore fresh combinations of enemies, abilities, and environments.

2. **Experiment with Breaker Classes and Abilities**: Don't settle for the first class and build you pick. The game encourages experimentation, and each Breaker class offers a unique way to approach combat. You might prefer a fast, aggressive style or a more strategic, ranged approach. Mix and match abilities and weapons to find what works best for you.

3. **Use Your Environment**: The world of *Hyper Light Breaker* is more than just a backdrop. Pay attention

to the environment—whether it's using elevation to your advantage in combat or finding hidden paths that lead to valuable loot. The more you explore, the more you'll discover.

4. **Co-op Is Your Friend**: If you're playing with friends, remember that teamwork makes the dream work. Don't rush ahead on your own—coordinate with your team to focus on roles, whether that's tanking damage, dealing damage, or providing support with abilities. Good communication is key to defeating the toughest regional bosses.

5. **Don't Forget the Hub City**: After each run, head back to the hub city. Here you'll find vital upgrades, NPCs, and a wealth of side activities that will make your next run even better. Keep an eye out for secrets and opportunities to improve your character.

6. **Focus on One Boss at a Time**: When you encounter regional bosses, focus your efforts on one at a time. While you might be tempted to rush through everything, each boss fight is a unique challenge that requires specific strategies. Don't spread yourself too thin—take your time and master one boss before moving on to the next.

7. **Patience Is Key**: As with any roguelike, *Hyper Light Breaker* rewards patience. You won't get everything on your first run, and that's okay. Learn from your mistakes, adapt, and return stronger each time. The more you play, the more the world will open up to you.

By following these tips, you'll not only be prepared for the game's challenges—you'll be on the path to mastery. This guide is here to ensure you're not just surviving but thriving in the world of *Hyper Light Breaker*. Every run is a chance to grow, and by the end, you'll look back at your journey with pride, knowing you've conquered everything the Overgrowth has to offer. Let's dive in, Breaker!

Chapter 1

Getting Started with *Hyper Light Breaker*

Overview of the Game and World

Hyper Light Breaker is a bold new chapter in the *Hyper Light* universe, continuing the legacy of *Hyper Light Drifter*, but with expansive new features, enhanced gameplay, and an ever-changing world. Developed by Heart Machine and published by Arc Games, *Hyper Light Breaker* brings together the vibrant and breathtaking world of Overgrowth, a hostile yet beautiful environment filled with secrets, powerful enemies, and regional bosses that challenge even the most seasoned players.

In this game, you play as a "Breaker," a skilled warrior who ventures into the Overgrowth with the ultimate goal of defeating the Abyss King. This central antagonist is a figure of immense power, and your task is to systematically defeat a series of regional bosses who guard the path to him. The game is set in a massive open world with biomes that are randomly generated with each new death. This ensures that each playthrough is unique, offering a fresh set of challenges, environments, and opportunities to explore.

The Overgrowth is a mystical world teeming with both beauty and danger. Unlike its predecessor, which was split into different levels, *Hyper Light Breaker* presents the entire world as a single interconnected space. It's not just about progressing through linear levels anymore; now, exploration and survival are at the heart of the experience.

The game uses a third-person perspective, allowing players to fully appreciate the sweeping landscapes and intricately designed environments. You'll traverse vast forests, climb sheer cliffs, explore ancient ruins, and navigate treacherous terrain in search of your next objective or enemy. Every corner hides a secret, whether it's an upgrade, a hidden passage, or an NPC who provides essential lore or quests.

One of the key features of *Hyper Light Breaker* is its roguelike element. Upon each death, the world is procedurally generated, meaning no two runs are ever exactly the same. This dynamic system encourages experimentation, as players can't rely on memorizing levels or strategies. Instead, they must adapt quickly and learn to survive in an ever-changing world.

The game also introduces multiplayer, allowing up to three players to team up and explore the world together. Cooperation is vital for success, as some enemies and bosses will require teamwork to defeat. Working with others allows players to combine abilities, share resources, and strategize together to overcome the toughest challenges.

The storytelling in *Hyper Light Breaker* is just as distinctive as its gameplay. There are no spoken dialogues in the game, similar to *Hyper Light Drifter*. Instead, the characters communicate through comic book-style panels, providing a visually rich and immersive experience. This allows for a more abstract and artistic method of storytelling, leaving room for interpretation and encouraging players to piece together the story themselves.

The game's world is divided into distinct biomes, each with its own set of challenges, environments, and enemies. As you journey through these biomes, you'll encounter powerful regional bosses, who guard the path to the Abyss King. Each boss is a unique challenge and will require careful planning, strategy, and execution to defeat.

But defeating bosses isn't the only goal in *Hyper Light Breaker*. The hub city between runs provides a place for you to regroup, explore, and plan your next moves. You can visit NPCs, unlock upgrades, and prepare for your next venture into the unpredictable world of Overgrowth.

First Steps: Basic Controls and Gameplay Mechanics

As a Breaker, you will need to master the basic controls and gameplay mechanics to survive and thrive in the hostile world of *Hyper Light Breaker*. In this section, we'll break down the core controls, combat mechanics, movement systems, and essential gameplay tips to get you started on the right foot.

Controls Overview

The controls in *Hyper Light Breaker* are designed to be fluid and responsive, allowing for fast-paced combat and smooth navigation of the world. Here's a breakdown of the essential controls:

- **Movement**:
  Use the left analog stick (on a controller) or the WASD keys (on a keyboard) to move your Breaker around the world. Movement is highly fluid, allowing for both fast traversal and controlled combat positioning. You'll want to make sure you're comfortable with basic movement before diving into the more complex mechanics.

- **Camera Control**:
  Use the right analog stick or mouse to control the camera. The third-person perspective gives you a clear view of your surroundings, which is crucial for both exploration and combat. Always keep an eye on your environment for hidden objects, enemies, and potential hazards.

- **Attack**:
  The standard attack button (R1 on controller / Left Mouse Button on PC) allows you to execute basic melee or ranged attacks. Depending on your Breaker class and abilities, these attacks can be combined in various ways to create powerful combos.

- **Dodge**:
  Dodging is an essential part of combat. Use the dodge button (Circle on controller / Spacebar on PC) to avoid enemy attacks, reposition yourself in battle, or escape dangerous situations. Timing your

dodges perfectly can make the difference between life and death, especially in boss fights.

- **Jump**:
  The jump button (X on controller / Spacebar on PC) lets you leap over obstacles, reach higher ground, or avoid ground-based attacks. This is essential for both combat and exploration.

- **Abilities**:
  Your Breaker comes with unique abilities that can be activated with specific buttons (L1 for controller / Q for PC). Abilities range from devastating attacks to supportive skills that enhance your survivability, such as shields or healing. Each ability can be customized and upgraded based on your playstyle.

- **Interact**:
  Use the interact button (Triangle on controller / E on PC) to interact with NPCs, objects, or lore items scattered around the world. Many hidden secrets and upgrades require you to interact with the environment to unlock them.

- **Hoverboard/Glider**:
  Movement becomes faster and more dynamic with the addition of the hoverboard and glider. Press the appropriate button (R2 on controller / Shift on PC) to activate these devices. The hoverboard is perfect for traversing large distances quickly, while the glider allows you to soar over large gaps and difficult terrain.

Core Gameplay Mechanics

- **Combat**:
  Combat is at the heart of *Hyper Light Breaker*, and understanding the basic mechanics is crucial for surviving the world of Overgrowth. In combat, you'll combine melee and ranged attacks, using the environment to your advantage and relying on your agility and abilities to outmaneuver enemies.

You'll face a variety of foes, from simple enemies that require basic strategies to massive regional bosses that demand careful planning and teamwork. Every attack has a purpose, and being able to quickly adapt to different enemies and combat scenarios is key to success.

Timing your dodges and using abilities at the right moments will determine whether you defeat enemies or end up respawning. There's a rhythm to combat in *Hyper Light Breaker*—learn to flow between dodging, attacking, and using your abilities.

- **Health and Resources**:
  You have a limited health pool, so managing your health and resources is essential. Health can be restored through pickups found in the environment, from defeated enemies, or by using specific abilities or items. Resources are required for upgrading weapons, abilities, and equipment. Be sure to keep an eye on your resource count and use them wisely.

- **Roguelike Elements**:
  Each death in *Hyper Light Breaker* results in the

world being procedurally generated anew, making each run unique. You'll never encounter the same exact world twice, which keeps the game feeling fresh and exciting. This also means you can't rely on memorizing the world's layout. Instead, you must rely on your skill, adaptability, and the knowledge gained from past runs.

Choosing Your Breaker: Classes, Abilities, and Playstyles

In *Hyper Light Breaker*, choosing the right class is crucial to your success. Each class has its own strengths and weaknesses, and how you build your Breaker will dictate your playstyle. Whether you prefer a melee-focused combat style, a ranged approach, or something more hybrid, the game provides flexibility to experiment and customize your character.

There are several Breaker classes to choose from, each offering distinct abilities and stats that influence how you approach both combat and exploration.

- **The Berserker**:
  This class focuses on heavy melee combat. The Berserker is a tanky, damage-dealing powerhouse that excels in close-range combat. You'll be able to use powerful swords and axes, smashing through enemies with ease. If you prefer to dive headfirst into the fray and deal massive damage, this is the class for you.

- **The Marksman**:
  The Marksman is all about precision and ranged attacks. With a focus on bows, crossbows, and firearms, the Marksman can deal damage from a distance while keeping enemies at bay. This class requires quick reflexes and careful aim, as your survivability depends on your ability to stay out of reach of enemies while dishing out damage.

- **The Engineer**:
  For players who enjoy versatility, the Engineer class provides a mix of both ranged and support abilities. Engineers can summon drones, deploy shields, and lay traps to control the battlefield. This class is ideal for players who like to manipulate the environment and use gadgets to gain an advantage over enemies.

- **The Sentinel**:
  The Sentinel is a balanced class, offering both defensive and offensive abilities. Equipped with a sword and shield, Sentinels can block incoming damage while also dealing decent melee damage. They are perfect for players who enjoy a strategic approach to combat, using their shield to block attacks while waiting for the perfect opportunity to strike.

Each Breaker class has a set of unique abilities that can be upgraded as you progress through the game. These abilities can range from offensive skills like explosive arrows to defensive buffs like shields that absorb damage. It's up to you to experiment and figure out which abilities complement your playstyle the most.

When selecting your Breaker class, consider the following:

- **Playstyle**: Do you prefer aggressive melee combat or ranged attacks? Do you want to be a tank that takes the hits, or a nimble fighter who stays out of danger?
- **Abilities**: Each class has different abilities that can drastically change your approach to combat. Make sure the abilities align with your preferred combat style.
- **Synergy with Multiplayer**: If you plan on playing in co-op mode, consider how your chosen class will synergize with your teammates. Some classes excel in solo combat but might need support when playing alongside others.

No matter which class you choose, you will be able to unlock and experiment with different builds and abilities as you progress through the game, allowing you to adapt to any challenge that the Overgrowth throws at you.

Chapter 2

Understanding the World of *Hyper Light Breaker*

The Overgrowth: Exploring the Vast World

In *Hyper Light Breaker*, the world you'll explore is unlike any other—vast, open, and brimming with danger and mystery. The Overgrowth, as it is called, is a dynamically generated, hostile environment where every corner hides both a threat and a potential reward. While the biomes you'll traverse might seem eerily familiar at first glance, they will constantly surprise you with new enemies, challenges, and areas to uncover. Each run in the Overgrowth offers a fresh perspective, providing new twists on the layout, obstacles, and adversaries. If you think you've mastered one area, the next time you step into it, everything might be completely different.

The Overgrowth is not simply a backdrop for your adventures; it is a character in its own right. The world of *Hyper Light Breaker* is alive with strange phenomena, weather conditions, and environmental storytelling that pulls you deeper into the experience. The landscape is marked by towering cliffs, vast forests, ancient ruins, and mechanized structures—all of which are connected by winding pathways and hidden passages. Despite its beauty, it is a treacherous world, filled with dangerous creatures, powerful bosses, and resource-hungry forces that will keep you on your toes.

The Biomes: Diversity in Environment and Challenge

The world of *Hyper Light Breaker* is divided into several biomes, each with its unique theme, enemies, and environmental hazards. These biomes contribute not only to the game's aesthetic appeal but also to its challenge and complexity. As you venture deeper into the Overgrowth, you will encounter various areas that challenge your skills in different ways. Whether you're scaling treacherous mountain ranges or battling in the depths of murky swamps, each biome is designed to push you to your limits.

- **The Verdant Wilds**: A lush, overgrown forest filled with vibrant plant life and mysterious fauna. The air is thick with the smell of damp earth, and the canopy above lets only dappled sunlight filter through. While it may look beautiful, it's a deadly place with hidden traps and aggressive wildlife lurking in the underbrush. Enemies here are fast and relentless, requiring you to remain vigilant and ready to dodge their attacks at a moment's notice.

- **The Ruined Stronghold**: This biome tells the story of a once-great civilization now reduced to broken ruins. Here, you'll find remnants of ancient technology, decaying walls, and forgotten artifacts. The challenge here comes from navigating through dense ruins and avoiding the mechanical defenses left behind by the civilization. Expect encounters with robotic enemies that vary from simple drones to large, imposing war machines that guard critical pathways.

- **The Blighted Swamps**: A murky, fog-filled area where visibility is limited and the ground is treacherous. It's an eerie, unsettling biome, home to the most dangerous and hostile creatures in the Overgrowth. Poisonous waters, quicksand, and venomous beasts await the unwary. Navigating through this area requires both careful planning and the ability to adapt quickly to changing conditions. Keep an eye on your stamina here, as the thick mud and swampy terrain will slow your movements considerably.

- **The Shattered Peaks**: A high-altitude region with towering cliffs and precarious paths. The air is thin, and your movements will be slower compared to lower-altitude areas. The wind howls as it blows across jagged rocks, creating unstable conditions for climbing and movement. Combat here can be particularly challenging, as enemies can knock you off the cliffs, and you'll need to be strategic to avoid falling.

- **The Hollowed Depths**: A subterranean biome filled with twisted caverns and dark, oppressive tunnels. The underground world is full of secrets and danger, with its tight corridors and hidden chambers. The enemies here are not only fierce but also rely on the darkness to their advantage, making it harder to spot them before they attack. The environment is claustrophobic, adding an additional layer of tension to every encounter.

Each biome serves as a backdrop to the gameplay, but also as an interactive challenge. The terrain you traverse and the enemies you face will require you to adapt and strategize accordingly. You will need to learn the lay of the land, the patterns of the creatures you'll face, and the tricks the environment plays to successfully navigate and survive.

Environmental Storytelling: A World with History

The Overgrowth is also rich with environmental storytelling. You won't find long narrative dialogues or verbose exposition, as *Hyper Light Breaker* follows in the footsteps of its predecessor, *Hyper Light Drifter*, with its minimalist approach to storytelling. Instead of words, the story is told through visual cues, environmental design, and the scattered remnants of past civilizations.

Every corner you turn could hold a piece of the world's history. Crumbled statues, ancient relics, and mysterious structures all hint at a forgotten past. You'll learn about the downfall of previous civilizations, the rise of new threats, and the motivations of key figures—all through subtle visual cues that draw you into the world. The lack of direct dialogue means that much of the story is left for the player to interpret, providing a rich, immersive experience where discovery is a reward in itself.

Movement Mechanics: Hoverboards, Gliders, and Wall Climbing

To traverse the vast and varied landscapes of the Overgrowth, you'll need more than just your legs. Movement in *Hyper Light Breaker* is designed to be fast, fluid, and dynamic, giving you the freedom to explore every corner of the world. The game offers several movement mechanics that allow you to travel efficiently, overcome obstacles, and maintain the game's pacing.

Hoverboards: Speed Across the World

Hoverboards are one of the most exciting additions to *Hyper Light Breaker*'s movement mechanics. As a Breaker, you can summon a hoverboard at any time to traverse the large distances between objectives quickly. These sleek, futuristic vehicles allow you to glide over the terrain, taking advantage of the open-world design and offering a fast-paced way to move between regions. Hoverboards come with their own set of challenges, though—they require skill to maneuver, especially when you're racing through dangerous biomes or avoiding enemy attacks.

Using the hoverboard isn't just about speed—it's also about style. You'll need to learn how to control your movement on the board, making sure to avoid obstacles, cliffs, and enemies. The terrain in *Hyper Light Breaker* isn't always flat, and the hoverboard's mechanics are designed to make even simple traversal feel exhilarating. Whether you're zooming through dense forests or skating across the edge of a cliff, mastering the hoverboard is an essential part of your exploration toolkit.

Hoverboards are also critical when it comes to exploring hidden areas and reaching hard-to-access places. You'll need to carefully control your hoverboard to glide over obstacles or make jumps across gaps in the world. A successful hoverboard run requires practice and precision, but it's one of the most rewarding ways to experience the world's vastness.

Gliders: Soar Above the World

In addition to hoverboards, gliders provide an added layer of mobility, allowing you to soar above the world and reach areas that would otherwise be impossible to access. When activated, the glider allows you to glide gracefully through the air, gaining elevation and crossing large gaps with ease. The glider is perfect for navigating high-altitude areas, making it an indispensable tool when exploring biomes like the Shattered Peaks or when trying to reach distant landmarks.

Controlling the glider requires a delicate balance. You need to manage your altitude and speed while navigating through strong winds or avoiding incoming hazards. The glider also requires fuel, which means you'll need to plan your route carefully and manage your resources to avoid running out of flight time. In some cases, you'll need to find special locations to recharge your glider or collect power-ups that will allow you to glide for longer distances.

Mastering the glider is essential for getting around the world efficiently and uncovering hidden treasures. You can use it to gain an aerial advantage in combat as well, positioning yourself above enemies and attacking from a safe distance. However, be warned: enemies in the Overgrowth are clever and will try to knock you out of the sky if you're not careful.

Wall Climbing: Overcoming Verticality

Not every part of the world is easily accessible with a hoverboard or glider. The Overgrowth is filled with sheer cliffs, tall buildings, and towering structures that demand a more hands-on approach. Wall climbing is a vital movement mechanic that allows you to scale vertical surfaces and access hidden areas high above the ground.

Wall climbing is intuitive but requires you to time your movements carefully. You can grab onto certain surfaces and use your climbing abilities to scale walls, jump between ledges, and find your way up to unreachable places. The climbing system in *Hyper Light Breaker* adds another layer of depth to exploration, as it opens up a variety of paths that wouldn't be accessible otherwise.

You can also combine wall climbing with other movement mechanics. For example, you might climb up a wall to reach a vantage point, then use your glider to soar to a distant platform. The combination of wall climbing with hoverboards and gliders gives you nearly unlimited freedom to explore every corner of the Overgrowth, ensuring that no part of the world is off-limits.

Random World Generation: What to Expect and How to Prepare

One of the defining features of *Hyper Light Breaker* is its roguelike system, which generates a new world each time you die. This means that no two runs are alike. Every time you venture into the Overgrowth, you'll face a fresh, unpredictable environment filled with new challenges, enemies, and objectives.

Procedural Generation: A Dynamic, Ever-Changing World

Procedural generation is a key aspect of the game's design, ensuring that players cannot rely on memorization or predefined paths. The world is generated randomly with each death, meaning that while the core structure remains the same—biomes, enemies, and bosses—the specific layout and composition of each run will always differ.

This dynamic world design encourages experimentation. You will encounter different enemies, terrain, and obstacles with each playthrough, which forces you to adapt your strategy and approach. What works in one run may not work in the next, so you'll need to think on your feet and adjust to the changing conditions.

Procedural generation also ensures replayability. Because each world is different, players can return to the game time and time again without feeling like they're experiencing the same thing over and over. The randomness injects a sense of excitement and discovery into every session.

How to Prepare for Random World Generation

Adapting to the game's roguelike nature requires preparation. Here are a few tips for making the most of the procedural generation system:

- **Learn the Core Mechanics**: The more you understand the basic gameplay mechanics, the easier it will be to adapt to new challenges. Familiarize yourself with combat, movement, and class abilities, as these will be essential in any environment.

- **Focus on Flexibility**: Since you can't predict the world layout, it's essential to be adaptable. Build your Breaker with a variety of skills and abilities that allow you to tackle different situations. Whether it's melee, ranged, or defensive abilities, having a versatile arsenal will give you an edge.

- **Explore Thoroughly**: Every run is an opportunity to uncover new secrets. Make sure you explore each area carefully, as you may stumble upon hidden treasures, upgrades, or lore that can help you on future runs.

- **Stay Calm and Strategize**: In *Hyper Light Breaker*, patience and strategic thinking are key. Don't panic when you encounter new challenges—take the time to evaluate the situation, analyze enemy patterns, and think through your options before making a move.

Chapter 3

Combat and Weapons in *Hyper Light Breaker*

In *Hyper Light Breaker*, combat is not just a series of button presses; it's an intricate dance of strategy, precision, and skill. Whether you are tearing through enemies with your melee weapon, picking off foes from a distance with your ranged arsenal, or mixing both styles to adapt to each encounter, mastering combat is essential for surviving the dangerous world of Overgrowth. This section will provide an in-depth look at how to master both melee and ranged combat, the best weapon combinations for various playstyles, expert combat tips, and strategies for managing your health, energy, and resources during intense battles.

Mastering Melee and Ranged Combat

Hyper Light Breaker allows you to approach combat in multiple ways, giving you the flexibility to tailor your fighting style to your preferences. Whether you prefer to get up close and personal with enemies or maintain a safe distance while picking them off from afar, the game offers both melee and ranged combat mechanics that are designed to be engaging and rewarding.

Melee Combat: Close Quarters, Powerful Strikes

Melee combat in *Hyper Light Breaker* is fast-paced, fluid, and dynamic. It involves timing, positioning, and mastering the rhythm of each weapon to defeat enemies. Whether you're wielding a sword, axe, or other close-range weapons, your ability to react to enemy movements and adapt to their attack patterns is key to success.

- **Weapon Types**: Melee weapons come in various forms, each offering a different combat experience. Here are the primary types of melee weapons you'll encounter:
  - **Swords**: Fast, agile, and versatile, swords are great for players who like to quickly move between enemies, delivering rapid strikes while evading counterattacks. They allow for quick combos and excellent mobility, making them perfect for aggressive playstyles that prioritize speed and agility.
  - **Axes**: These heavy-hitting weapons are slower but deal massive damage with each swing. Axes are ideal for players who prefer to focus on single-target damage, especially during boss fights. With the right timing, you can deal devastating blows that can break through enemy defenses and stagger foes.
  - **Polearms**: These long-range melee weapons give you the ability to control space, making them ideal for keeping enemies at bay. They

offer a mix of speed and range, allowing you to strike from a safe distance while maintaining control of the battlefield. Polearms are especially effective when fighting multiple enemies at once.

- o **Fists/Claws**: For players who enjoy up-close brawling, using claws or fists allows you to land rapid punches, making this a more high-risk, high-reward weapon choice. They excel at fast, relentless combat, but you'll need to be skilled at dodging and positioning yourself to avoid enemy attacks.

- **Combo Attacks and Flow**: The key to mastering melee combat in *Hyper Light Breaker* is learning how to chain attacks together effectively. Each weapon has its own set of combo attacks that can be strung together to maximize damage. Mastering the flow of these attacks will allow you to perform devastating combos that leave your enemies with little time to react.

    - o **Basic Combos**: Start by learning basic combos with your chosen weapon, which will serve as the foundation for more complex chains. Whether it's a simple three-hit combo or a single strong blow followed by a quick follow-up, your understanding of timing is essential.

    - o **Advanced Combos**: As you progress, you'll unlock more advanced combo attacks. These can include special moves that knock enemies back, deal elemental damage, or stun enemies long enough for you to deliver a finishing blow. Experiment with these advanced moves to find what best suits your playstyle.

Ranged Combat: Precision and Distance

Ranged combat is just as essential in *Hyper Light Breaker* as melee combat. With the right ranged weapon, you can take out enemies before they even get close, allowing you to control the pace of the fight from a distance. Whether you're using bows, guns, or energy-based weapons, ranged combat rewards precision, timing, and adaptability.

- **Weapon Types**: In *Hyper Light Breaker*, you can equip a variety of ranged weapons, each suited to different combat scenarios. The primary ranged weapons include:
    - **Bows**: The bow is a classic ranged weapon, offering both precision and flexibility. It allows you to fire arrows at enemies from a distance, dealing moderate damage while giving you time to dodge and reposition. The bow excels at targeting weak spots on enemies and is ideal for players who prefer a more tactical approach to combat.
    - **Crossbows**: Similar to bows, crossbows pack more punch and have a slower reload time. While they may not offer the speed of

a bow, they make up for it with higher damage output per shot. The crossbow is perfect for players who want to focus on single-shot damage and taking down high-priority targets from a distance.

- **Energy Weapons**: These high-tech weapons fire energy blasts that deal significant damage. They are especially effective against mechanical enemies and can sometimes even penetrate armor. While they require energy to use, they can be extremely powerful when used strategically, as they allow you to engage enemies from a safe distance without worrying about reload times.
- **Firearms**: Firearms, such as pistols or rifles, offer high-speed firing capabilities and rapid damage output. They are great for close-quarters ranged combat and allow you to lay down suppressing fire while repositioning. Firearms are useful in situations where you need to deal consistent damage quickly.

- **Aiming and Positioning**: Mastering ranged combat is about more than just firing at enemies. Precision and positioning are critical. Use cover to protect yourself while you line up shots, and take advantage of high ground or environmental features that give you a clear shot. Many enemies have weak spots that can be exploited with ranged attacks, so keep an eye out for areas to target for maximum damage.

- **Ammo Management**: Many ranged weapons in *Hyper Light Breaker* require ammo or energy, so it's important to manage your resources effectively. Running out of ammo during a fight can leave you vulnerable, so always make sure you have enough supplies before engaging in a major battle. Keep an eye on your ammo count and take advantage of opportunities to restock during exploration.

Best Weapon Combinations for Different Playstyles

The beauty of *Hyper Light Breaker* is the freedom it offers players to tailor their combat experience to their preferred playstyle. Whether you want to go all-in on melee combat, take a more tactical ranged approach, or mix and match both styles, the game offers multiple weapon combinations that allow you to adapt to different situations. Here are a few optimal weapon combinations based on different playstyles:

1. The Balanced Playstyle: Sword + Bow

For players who want a bit of everything, a combination of a fast, agile sword with a ranged bow provides balance and flexibility. The sword allows you to quickly dispatch enemies in close quarters, while the bow lets you target foes from a distance.

- **Why it Works**: The sword's fast attack speed and combo potential complement the bow's precision and range. You can clear out mobs with your sword while using the bow to pick off high-priority enemies or target weak spots from afar.

- **Playstyle Tips**: The key to this playstyle is adapting to the situation. When fighting groups of enemies, you can use the sword to take them out quickly. When facing a tough boss or a powerful enemy, switch to the bow to maintain a safe distance while dealing consistent damage.

2. The Heavy-Hitter Playstyle: Axe + Energy Weapon

If you prefer raw power and devastating single-target damage, the combination of an axe and an energy weapon is perfect for you. The axe's heavy hits are excellent for breaking through enemy defenses, while the energy weapon offers long-range damage for those moments when you need to stay at a distance.

- **Why it Works**: The axe delivers massive damage in close-range combat, allowing you to break through enemy defenses and stagger tougher foes. Meanwhile, the energy weapon gives you the ability to deal substantial damage from afar without worrying about reload times.

- **Playstyle Tips**: Use the axe in close-range combat for crowd control and high-damage output. When you need to avoid taking damage or fight enemies at range, switch to the energy weapon and keep your distance.

3. The Stealth and Precision Playstyle: Crossbow + Polearm

For players who enjoy a more tactical, precision-based approach, a crossbow combined with a polearm is a perfect choice. The crossbow allows you to deal high-damage shots from a distance, while the polearm offers versatility in both melee combat and crowd control.

- **Why it Works**: The crossbow's ability to deal heavy damage with a single shot, paired with the polearm's reach and speed, allows you to take out enemies before they get too close. You can use the polearm to control space and keep enemies at a distance, while the crossbow takes care of high-priority targets.
- **Playstyle Tips**: Use the polearm for keeping enemies at bay and handling multiple foes at once. When you spot a dangerous target or a tough boss, switch to the crossbow and take them out from a safe distance.

Combat Tips: How to Take Down Enemies Efficiently

Mastering combat in *Hyper Light Breaker* is about more than just knowing your weapon combos—it's about adapting to different enemies, understanding their attack patterns, and using your environment to your advantage. Here are some key combat tips to help you take down enemies efficiently:

1. Learn Enemy Patterns

Every enemy in *Hyper Light Breaker* has a set of attack patterns. Understanding these patterns is crucial for evading damage and counterattacking effectively. Some enemies may charge at you, others might use ranged attacks, while some may perform devastating area-of-effect (AoE) moves. By learning these patterns, you can anticipate their attacks and position yourself to strike back.

- **Tip**: Pay attention to enemy tells. Many enemies will give you a visual cue before they attack, such as raising an arm before a heavy strike or winding up for a ranged shot. Use these cues to dodge or block effectively.

2. Master Dodging and Positioning

Dodging is one of your most essential tools in combat. Being able to dodge enemy attacks and reposition yourself during a fight can make the difference between life and death. Use your dodge to avoid incoming damage, get behind enemies, or create distance when necessary.

- **Tip**: Always keep your distance from enemies with powerful AoE attacks or long-range projectiles. Use your dodge to move in and out of range quickly, striking when it's safe and retreating when you need to.

3. Use the Environment to Your Advantage

The Overgrowth is filled with environmental features that can help you during combat. Whether it's taking cover behind rocks to avoid ranged attacks or using high ground to gain an advantage over enemies, the environment plays a significant role in your combat strategy.

- **Tip**: Use the terrain to block enemy attacks or create obstacles between you and ranged enemies.

> High ground often gives you a better vantage point and allows you to fire from a distance while avoiding melee enemies.

4. Combine Abilities with Weapon Attacks

Many Breaker classes have abilities that can complement their weapon attacks, such as defensive shields, healing abilities, or elemental damage boosts. Combining these abilities with your weapon attacks can significantly improve your combat efficiency.

- **Tip**: Use your abilities strategically—don't just spam them. For example, activating a shield ability before diving into melee combat with a powerful enemy can give you the upper hand, while a damage-boosting ability can help you take down a tough boss much faster.

Managing Health, Energy, and Resources During Fights

Fights in *Hyper Light Breaker* are resource-intensive. Whether it's managing your health, keeping an eye on your energy levels for abilities, or ensuring you have enough ammo for ranged combat, resource management is key to surviving and thriving in battle.

1. Health Management

Your health is one of your most important resources, and managing it effectively is essential during combat. Health can be restored through pickups, abilities, and certain weapons or items, but you need to be strategic in how you use it.

- **Tip**: Keep track of your health at all times. If you're low on health, don't be afraid to retreat and look for pickups. Many enemies drop healing items when defeated, so make sure to explore thoroughly and grab anything that can restore your health.

2. Energy Management

Energy is used to activate special abilities, which can turn the tide of battle in your favor. Managing your energy efficiently is just as important as managing your health, as running out of energy can leave you vulnerable in the middle of a fight.

- **Tip**: Conserve energy during regular combat, and only use abilities when necessary. Focus on taking down enemies efficiently, and save your energy for boss fights or tougher enemies where abilities will make the most difference.

3. Resource Management

In addition to health and energy, you'll need to manage resources like ammo, crafting materials, and upgrades. Running out of resources during a fight can leave you at a disadvantage.

- **Tip**: Always keep an eye on your ammo count and make sure to restock when you can. Additionally, upgrade your weapons and abilities regularly to ensure you're always prepared for tougher challenges.

Chapter 4

The Role of Abilities and Classes in *Hyper Light Breaker*

In *Hyper Light Breaker*, your chosen class and abilities play a critical role in shaping your combat style, exploration efficiency, and overall success in the world of Overgrowth. The game offers a diverse selection of Breaker classes, each with its unique abilities and strengths, allowing you to tailor your gameplay experience to match your preferred style. Whether you enjoy rushing into combat with brute force or favor a tactical approach that relies on ranged attacks and strategic positioning, *Hyper Light Breaker* provides you with the tools you need to succeed. This section will break down the different Breaker classes, the key abilities they offer, and provide guidance on how to build and customize your Breaker for maximum effectiveness.

Breakdown of Breaker Classes

Each class in *Hyper Light Breaker* offers a distinct approach to combat, providing players with unique strategies, strengths, and weaknesses. Understanding the core functions of each class is essential to picking the one that aligns with your playstyle. Let's take a look at the different Breaker classes available in the game.

1. The Berserker

The Berserker is a close-quarters combat specialist who excels at dealing massive damage with heavy melee weapons. This class is designed for players who love to charge into battle headfirst, taking down enemies with powerful strikes while absorbing damage. If you enjoy high-risk, high-reward combat, the Berserker is the ideal class for you.

- **Strengths**: The Berserker has high health and strong melee damage, making them a powerhouse in close combat. They can sustain themselves in prolonged fights and deal heavy damage to enemies.

- **Weaknesses**: Due to the focus on melee combat, the Berserker can be vulnerable to ranged enemies or larger groups of foes. They rely on close proximity to deal effective damage, which means positioning and timing are crucial.

- **Recommended Playstyle**: The Berserker excels in aggressive, high-damage combat. Charge in and deal heavy blows with your axe or sword, taking advantage of your health pool to absorb hits. You'll need to stay close to enemies and use your superior damage output to clear out foes quickly.

2. The Marksman

The Marksman is the master of ranged combat. Armed with bows, crossbows, and firearms, the Marksman specializes in taking down enemies from a distance. This class is perfect for players who prefer precision, strategy, and hitting enemies from afar.

- **Strengths**: The Marksman can deal consistent, high-damage shots from a distance. Their weapons excel at picking off enemies one by one, making them effective in controlling space during combat. They can target weak points and take down enemies before they get close.

- **Weaknesses**: The Marksman is vulnerable in close-quarters combat. If enemies close the distance too quickly, the Marksman may struggle to fend them off without proper positioning or backup.

- **Recommended Playstyle**: For the Marksman, mobility is key. Keep your distance from enemies, use cover to line up precise shots, and take advantage of the long-range capabilities of your weapons. Focus on picking off threats one by one, avoiding combat at close range unless absolutely necessary.

3. The Engineer

The Engineer is a versatile class that excels at supporting teammates and controlling the battlefield. With the ability to deploy drones, turrets, and other tech-based devices, the Engineer is a well-rounded class suited for both offensive and defensive play. This class is ideal for players who enjoy using gadgets and environmental manipulation to turn the tide of battle.

- **Strengths**: The Engineer is highly adaptable, with abilities that can heal, shield, and deal damage. The class's unique ability to summon support devices, like turrets and drones, allows the Engineer to create chaos for enemies while supporting their team.

- **Weaknesses**: While the Engineer can deal decent damage, they are not as specialized in either melee or ranged combat. The class relies on their gadgets to do most of the heavy lifting, which means their effectiveness is tied to how well their equipment is utilized.

- **Recommended Playstyle**: The Engineer should focus on supporting their team while dealing moderate damage. Use your drones and turrets to control space, provide healing or shields for allies, and add additional firepower in combat. Position yourself in a way that maximizes your gadgets' effectiveness, while also staying safe in the backline when necessary.

4. The Sentinel

The Sentinel is the tank of *Hyper Light Breaker*, designed to absorb damage and protect allies while dealing decent melee damage. Armed with shields and defensive abilities, the Sentinel can withstand heavy hits while controlling the battlefield with crowd control and support skills. If you prefer a more strategic, team-oriented approach to combat, the Sentinel is the right class for you.

- **Strengths**: The Sentinel has excellent defensive capabilities, making them resilient to damage. Their shield allows them to block incoming attacks, while their melee attacks can deal solid damage to enemies. The Sentinel is perfect for drawing aggro and protecting weaker allies in multiplayer sessions.

- **Weaknesses**: The Sentinel can struggle to deal massive damage compared to other classes, especially against fast-moving enemies. They rely on their shield and positioning to stay effective, so careful management of their defensive resources is key.

- **Recommended Playstyle**: Play as a frontline tank who engages enemies head-on, protecting allies and controlling the pace of battle. Use your shield to block incoming damage, and make sure you're positioning yourself between enemies and your teammates. The Sentinel excels in team-based combat, so work with your allies to hold the line while you deal steady damage.

Key Abilities and Their Impact on Gameplay

Each Breaker class in *Hyper Light Breaker* has its own set of abilities that dramatically impact how you approach combat. These abilities provide unique advantages in battle, whether it's increasing your offensive power, providing support, or enhancing your mobility. Understanding the abilities available to each class and how to use them effectively is crucial for mastering your chosen playstyle.

1. Berserker Abilities

   - **Berserk Charge**: The Berserker charges forward with incredible speed, delivering a powerful strike that damages and knocks back enemies. This ability allows the Berserker to close the distance between themselves and enemies quickly, making it perfect for aggressive playstyles.

   - **Rage Unleashed**: Temporarily increases the Berserker's damage output and attack speed, turning them into a whirlwind of destruction. This ability is ideal for dealing with large groups of enemies or powerful bosses.

   - **Iron Will**: Grants the Berserker temporary invulnerability to damage for a short duration, allowing them to tank hits and keep fighting. This ability is essential for maintaining aggression in dangerous situations.

2. Marksman Abilities

   - **Precision Shot**: The Marksman lines up a perfect shot, dealing critical damage to a single target. This ability is perfect for picking off high-priority enemies from a distance and can be used to target weak spots on larger enemies.

   - **Explosive Arrow**: Fires an explosive arrow that deals area-of-effect (AoE) damage. Ideal for clearing out groups of enemies or damaging a cluster of foes hiding behind cover, this ability provides versatility to the Marksman's ranged combat.

- **Camouflage**: Temporarily renders the Marksman invisible to enemies, allowing for stealthy attacks or retreat. This ability is useful for avoiding combat when overwhelmed or setting up surprise attacks.

3. Engineer Abilities

- **Turret Deployment**: The Engineer can place an automated turret that targets and fires at enemies in the vicinity. This ability provides additional firepower during combat and is particularly useful for creating distractions or defending choke points.

- **Healing Drones**: Deploys drones that heal allies over time. This ability is great for supporting your team during prolonged fights, ensuring that everyone stays in fighting shape.

- **EMP Burst**: Releases a burst of electromagnetic energy that disables enemy technology and stuns mechanical enemies. This ability is essential for countering robotic foes and disabling enemy weapons or traps.

4. Sentinel Abilities

- **Shield Block**: The Sentinel can raise their shield to block incoming damage, absorbing the impact of enemy attacks. This ability allows the Sentinel to stay in the fight longer and protect weaker teammates.

- **Ground Slam**: The Sentinel slams their shield into the ground, causing a shockwave that damages and stuns nearby enemies. This ability is useful for crowd control, disrupting enemy formations, and creating opportunities for teammates to attack.
- **Taunt**: The Sentinel forces nearby enemies to focus their attacks on them, drawing aggro away from their allies. This ability is essential for tanking and ensuring that your teammates remain safe during combat.

How to Build and Customize Your Breaker for Success

Customizing your Breaker's build and abilities is a crucial part of achieving success in *Hyper Light Breaker*. The game offers various ways to enhance your character, ensuring that your chosen class fits your preferred playstyle. Here's how you can build your Breaker for maximum effectiveness:

1. Weapon Synergy with Abilities

Choosing the right combination of weapons and abilities is vital for creating a cohesive and effective Breaker build. While some weapons and abilities naturally complement each other, it's important to experiment with different combinations to find what works best for your playstyle.

- **Berserker Build**: If you prefer to focus on raw melee damage, pair the Berserker class with an axe or polearm. The Berserker's abilities, like **Rage**

Unleashed and **Iron Will**, synergize perfectly with heavy-hitting weapons, allowing you to deal massive damage while tanking hits.

- **Marksman Build**: For long-range combat, pair the Marksman with a bow or crossbow. Use abilities like **Precision Shot** to target weak spots and **Camouflage** to remain undetected while setting up your attacks.

- **Engineer Build**: The Engineer excels when used as a support character. Pair them with a versatile weapon, such as a rifle, and focus on abilities like **Healing Drones** and **Turret Deployment** to ensure that your team stays alive while dealing consistent damage.

- **Sentinel Build**: The Sentinel thrives in tanking and crowd control. Pair them with a sword or shield and focus on abilities like **Shield Block** and **Taunt** to absorb damage while protecting your teammates.

2. Ability Upgrades

As you progress through *Hyper Light Breaker*, you'll be able to upgrade your abilities, making them even more powerful. Consider how you want to build your Breaker when selecting upgrades.

- **Focus on Core Abilities**: Upgrade the abilities that match your preferred playstyle. If you're a Berserker, focus on upgrading **Rage Unleashed** to maximize damage. If you're playing a Marksman, upgrading **Explosive Arrow** can increase your ability to deal AoE damage.

- **Prioritize Survivability**: Regardless of your class, prioritize upgrading abilities that enhance your survivability. Abilities that provide healing, shields, or damage mitigation are essential for staying alive during difficult fights.

- **Experiment with Different Builds**: Don't be afraid to experiment with different ability upgrades as you progress. Some abilities may work better for certain biomes or enemy types, so feel free to adjust your build depending on the situation.

3. Resource Management and Gear Customization

Managing your resources—such as health, energy, and ammo—is a critical aspect of your build. Additionally, customizing your gear with upgrades and enhancements can make a significant difference in your combat performance.

- **Focus on Resource Generation**: Look for gear and abilities that help generate or conserve energy, health, and ammo. The more you can manage these resources, the longer you can stay in the fight.

- **Gear Synergy**: Choose gear that complements your abilities. For example, if you're playing a tanky Sentinel, prioritize armor and shield upgrades. If you're a Marksman, look for gear that boosts your ranged damage or gives you extra ammo capacity.

By understanding your class's strengths and customizing your abilities and gear, you'll be able to maximize your effectiveness in combat and tailor your gameplay to suit your preferred playstyle.

Chapter 5

Boss Battles: Defeat the Regional Bosses in *Hyper Light Breaker*

Boss battles in *Hyper Light Breaker* are where the game truly tests your skills, offering challenges that require precise tactics, adaptability, and mastery of the game's mechanics. Each regional boss you face is unique, with distinct attack patterns, weaknesses, and environmental factors that demand careful preparation and a keen sense of timing. Whether you're fighting solo or with friends in multiplayer mode, each boss encounter is a monumental event that tests your ability to strategize, coordinate, and execute.

This section will walk you through essential preparation tips for boss battles, provide detailed walkthroughs for each regional boss, and offer special multiplayer tactics to help you succeed in these challenging encounters.

Preparing for Boss Fights: Essential Tips and Strategies

Before diving into any boss fight, preparation is key. Bosses in *Hyper Light Breaker* are not only tough but often introduce new mechanics or environmental challenges that require you to think on your feet. Here are some essential preparation tips to ensure you're ready for the battle ahead:

1. Know Your Boss

Each regional boss has its own unique attack patterns, strengths, and weaknesses. It's essential to learn as much as possible about the boss before engaging in the fight. Here are some general steps to take:

- **Research the Boss**: If you're playing in single-player mode, be sure to read any in-game lore or encounter notes that provide information about the boss. This may include hints on weaknesses, attack patterns, and suggested strategies.

- **Study Attack Patterns**: During your first encounter, focus on observing the boss's attacks rather than rushing in. Each boss will have a series of predictable moves—some are easier to dodge, while others may require more careful positioning.

2. Prepare Your Gear and Abilities

Boss fights often require you to adapt your build to the specific encounter. Make sure your gear and abilities are suited for the battle.

- **Gear Up for the Fight**: Equip your Breaker with the best weapons and armor available. Consider bringing weapons that exploit the boss's weaknesses (e.g., elemental damage against a boss vulnerable to fire or ice).

- **Ability Synergy**: Choose abilities that help you counter the boss's attacks. For example, if the boss has powerful area-of-effect (AoE) attacks, equip defensive abilities like shields or mobility boosts to avoid getting hit. Healing or regeneration abilities are also crucial, as they allow you to sustain yourself during the battle.

3. Stock Up on Resources

Boss battles are resource-intensive. Before the fight, make sure you have ample supplies of healing items, energy boosts, and any other resources that will give you an edge in the fight.

- **Health and Energy**: Have healing items readily available to restore your health during the fight. Energy boosters are also essential for ensuring you can use your abilities when needed. Plan to manage your health and energy efficiently, especially in longer boss battles.
- **Ammo for Ranged Combat**: If you're using ranged weapons like bows or crossbows, ensure you have a sufficient supply of ammo. Running out of ammo in the middle of a fight can leave you vulnerable and unprepared.

4. Utilize the Environment

Many boss fights take place in environments that can provide you with tactical advantages. Look for cover, high ground, or other elements of the environment that you can use to avoid damage, gain an advantage in combat, or find weak spots in the boss's defense.

- **Cover**: Use walls or other structures to hide behind when the boss is charging up an AoE attack or ranged shot. These environmental features can serve as vital protection when you need to recover or wait for an opportunity to strike.
- **Positioning**: Boss arenas are often designed with specific mechanics in mind, such as narrow walkways or platforms. Use the environment to control the flow of the battle, positioning yourself on high ground or using space to keep the boss at a distance.

5. Know When to Retreat

Sometimes, the best strategy is to retreat and regroup. If you find yourself overwhelmed or on the brink of defeat, it's okay to back off, heal, and reassess your strategy. Knowing when to retreat is just as important as knowing when to fight.

Regional Boss Walkthroughs: How to Defeat Each Boss

Every regional boss in *Hyper Light Breaker* has its own set of challenges. Below is a breakdown of how to approach some of the toughest bosses in the game, including their attack patterns, strategies for defeating them, and tips for handling each fight.

1. The Verdant Guardian

The Verdant Guardian is the first major boss you will encounter in *Hyper Light Breaker*. This powerful creature, resembling a giant, mutated plant, resides in the lush Verdant Wilds biome. It combines physical attacks with poison-based projectiles, making this fight both a test of endurance and agility.

- **Attack Patterns**:
  - **Poison Spit**: The Verdant Guardian spits poison in a spread pattern. This attack is slow but can cover a wide area, so be prepared to dodge quickly.
  - **Charging Slam**: The Guardian will occasionally charge up a slam attack, causing massive damage in a radius around it.
  - **Summon Vines**: The Guardian can summon vines to entangle you. These vines slow your movement and deal damage over time, so it's important to avoid getting caught in them.
- **Strategy**:
  - **Dodge and Counter**: Use your agility to dodge the poison spit and charge slam attacks. After the charge slam, there's a brief moment when the Guardian is vulnerable. Rush in and land a few heavy hits during this time.

- **Use Ranged Attacks**: If you're playing as a Marksman or using ranged weapons, position yourself on high ground and pick off the Guardian from a distance to avoid getting too close to the vines.
- **Break the Vines**: When the Guardian summons vines, destroy them quickly to avoid getting trapped. Use a weapon with high AoE damage, such as an axe, to break the vines faster.

2. The Iron Colossus

The Iron Colossus is a mechanical boss that resides in the Ruined Stronghold biome. It has immense health, an array of devastating melee and ranged attacks, and a nearly impenetrable defense system.

- **Attack Patterns**:
    - **Melee Smash**: The Colossus swings its massive fists in wide arcs, dealing heavy damage to anything in its path.
    - **Rocket Barrage**: The Colossus launches a series of rockets, which track your movement and deal significant damage if they hit.
    - **Shield Charge**: It charges toward you, using its shield to knock you back and deal damage.
- **Strategy**:

- **Target Weak Spots**: The Iron Colossus has weak points on its back and under its arms. Focus your attacks on these spots to deal maximum damage. Use ranged weapons to exploit these weak points from a safe distance.

- **Dodge and Evade**: The Colossus' rocket barrage is deadly, but you can dodge them with precise timing. Keep an eye on its movements and be ready to use your dodge ability at the right moment to avoid the rockets.

- **Use Mobility**: Use your hoverboard or glider to avoid the Colossus' charge attacks and maintain a safe distance while dealing damage.

3. The Abyss Serpent

The Abyss Serpent is one of the toughest bosses in *Hyper Light Breaker*, encountered in the Blighted Swamps biome. It is a large, serpentine creature that strikes with deadly precision and can manipulate the swamp's waters to its advantage.

- **Attack Patterns**:
  - **Water Jets**: The Serpent fires high-pressure jets of water from its mouth, pushing you back and dealing damage.

- **Tentacle Slam**: It summons massive tentacles from the swamp floor, which slam down and cause AoE damage.
- **Venomous Bites**: The Serpent will occasionally attempt to bite you, causing both direct damage and poisoning.

- **Strategy**:
  - **Dodge and Recover**: The Abyss Serpent's water jets can knock you off platforms or disrupt your positioning. Dodge to avoid being pushed into dangerous areas, and retreat if necessary to recover.
  - **Aim for the Head**: While attacking the tentacles is effective for crowd control, focus your main damage on the Serpent's head. Use your ranged weapons to hit the Serpent from a distance, aiming for its vulnerable head when it rears up.
  - **Use the Environment**: The Blighted Swamps offer some cover and high ground, so use these features to protect yourself from the Serpent's attacks. Be aware of the swamp's slow-moving waters, as they can hinder your movement.

Special Tactics for Multiplayers in Boss Fights

Boss fights in *Hyper Light Breaker* become even more exciting (and challenging) when you bring friends into the fold. Multiplayer combat offers a host of new strategies and tactical possibilities, but it also requires coordination, communication, and careful planning to succeed.

1. Divide and Conquer

In multiplayer, dividing the team into specialized roles is key. You'll want to assign certain players to focus on dealing damage, others on providing support, and some on tanking or distracting the boss.

- **DPS (Damage Dealers)**: These players should focus on hitting the boss with as much damage as possible, whether from melee or ranged attacks. Make sure these players stay mobile and avoid getting hit too often.

- **Tanks**: Tanks should focus on drawing the boss's attention and absorbing damage. The Sentinel is an ideal class for this role, as their taunt abilities allow them to control enemy aggro. The tank should always position themselves between the boss and the rest of the team.

- **Support**: Support players should focus on healing, providing shields, and using abilities that can disable the boss or buff the team. Engineers excel in this role, with abilities like drones and turrets offering assistance during the fight.

2. Synchronize Abilities

In multiplayer boss fights, the coordination of abilities is vital for success. Make sure your team is aware of when certain abilities should be used, such as healing abilities, buffs, or defensive shields.

- **Timing**: Timing your abilities is crucial. For example, if a boss is about to unleash a devastating AoE attack, have the support players use shields or healing abilities just before the attack lands to mitigate damage.

- **Combos**: Certain abilities can be combined for maximum effectiveness. A coordinated combo of damage-dealing abilities can quickly bring down a boss's health, while a well-timed stun or debuff can make a boss more vulnerable to attacks.

Chapter 6

The Abyss King: Your Final Challenge

The Abyss King is the ultimate challenge in *Hyper Light Breaker*. As the final boss of the game, he embodies everything you've learned throughout your journey—his immense power, unique abilities, and complex mechanics will test your skills in every possible way. The fight against the Abyss King is not just a test of strength but also of strategy, adaptability, and execution. In this section, we'll prepare you for this monumental battle, provide a detailed strategy for defeating the Abyss King, and offer expert tips for securing victory and completing the game.

Preparing for the Final Showdown

Before stepping into the Abyss King's domain, it's crucial to ensure you're fully prepared for the battle. This fight will demand everything you've learned and more, so preparation is key. Here's a checklist to ensure you're ready for the final confrontation:

1. Gear Up for Battle

The Abyss King is a formidable opponent, and your gear needs to reflect that. Your weapons, armor, and abilities should be optimized for both offense and defense. Here's what to prioritize:

- **Weapons**: Choose weapons that offer both high damage and versatility. A combination of a ranged weapon (such as a bow or crossbow) for dealing damage from a distance and a powerful melee weapon (like an axe or polearm) for close encounters is ideal. The Abyss King will engage in both ranged and close-quarters combat, so having a balanced weapon setup is crucial.

- **Armor**: Equip armor that maximizes your survivability. Focus on defensive stats that increase your health and reduce damage taken. The Abyss King's attacks can be devastating, so you'll need to be able to withstand his blows.

- **Abilities**: Abilities that enhance your damage output, mobility, and defensive capabilities are essential. Consider abilities that allow you to dodge or mitigate damage (such as shields or invincibility frames). You'll also want abilities that let you deal high damage during the brief moments of vulnerability in the Abyss King's attacks.

2. Stock Up on Resources

Boss battles are resource-heavy, and the Abyss King fight is no exception. Stock up on healing items, energy boosters, and any other resources that will help you during the battle. You'll need to keep your health topped off while also ensuring that you have enough energy to activate your most powerful abilities when necessary.

- **Healing Items**: Bring plenty of health potions or other healing items to restore your health when it dips. You'll want to ensure you can continue fighting without having to retreat for healing.

- **Energy Boosters**: Since you'll likely be using abilities throughout the fight, make sure you have energy boosters to keep your abilities available. Running out of energy during a critical moment could cost you the fight.

- **Ranged Ammo**: If you're using ranged weapons like a bow or crossbow, ensure you have ample ammo for the fight. You don't want to run out of projectiles during the battle, especially when attacking from a distance is crucial.

3. Learn the Arena

The arena where you fight the Abyss King is a key component of the battle. It's essential to familiarize yourself with the terrain and how it can impact the fight. The Abyss King's arena will have both advantageous and disadvantageous elements that you can use to your advantage:

- **Cover and Terrain**: Take note of any cover you can use to shield yourself from the Abyss King's ranged attacks. There may also be areas of the arena where you can gain higher ground to increase your damage potential, especially if you're using ranged weapons.

- **Environmental Hazards**: The arena may feature environmental hazards, such as lava pits, traps, or other obstacles. Be mindful of your surroundings, as the Abyss King may try to use these hazards against you. Stay aware of any changes in the arena as the fight progresses.

4. Prepare Mentally

The Abyss King is a challenging opponent, and the fight can be grueling. Make sure you're mentally prepared for a long and intense battle. Take breaks if you find yourself getting frustrated, and approach the fight with patience and adaptability. This is a battle that requires precision and timing, so don't rush.

Abyss King Boss Fight Strategy

The Abyss King is a dynamic and multi-phase boss with powerful attacks and unpredictable behaviors. To defeat him, you'll need to learn his attack patterns, recognize his vulnerabilities, and take advantage of moments when he's open to attack. Here's a step-by-step strategy for taking down the Abyss King:

Phase 1: The Abyss King's Opening Attacks

When the fight begins, the Abyss King will start with a series of basic attacks that can catch you off guard if you're not prepared. These attacks are powerful but relatively predictable.

- **Abyss Swipe**: The Abyss King swings his massive claws in wide arcs. These swipes deal significant damage and can knock you back if they land. To avoid this attack, keep your distance and time your dodges carefully. After the swipe, the Abyss King is momentarily vulnerable—this is your opportunity to land a few quick hits.

- **Abyss Fireball**: The Abyss King fires a slow-moving fireball from a distance, causing large AoE damage on impact. If you're using ranged weapons, try to shoot down the fireball before it reaches you. If it's too late, dodge to the side to avoid the blast radius.

- **Roar of the Abyss**: The Abyss King emits a powerful roar that stuns and disorients you. This is a dangerous attack that can leave you vulnerable to follow-up strikes. When you hear the roar, immediately use a shield or defensive ability to mitigate the stun effect, or use your dodge ability to get out of range.

Phase 2: Enraged Abyss King

After depleting the Abyss King's health by a certain percentage, he enters an enraged state. During this phase, his attacks become faster and more aggressive, and he gains access to new, devastating abilities.

- **Ground Slam**: The Abyss King slams his fists into the ground, creating shockwaves that travel across the arena. These shockwaves can damage you even if you're not directly under the Abyss King's fists. Watch for the wind-up and use your dodge ability to avoid the shockwaves.

- **Abyss Spikes**: The ground will erupt with spikes, creating temporary obstacles that can deal massive damage. During this phase, keep an eye on the ground for signs of incoming spikes and avoid standing in their paths. This adds a layer of complexity to the fight, requiring you to manage both the Abyss King's attacks and the environmental hazards.
- **Summon Minions**: The Abyss King will occasionally summon smaller minions that swarm you while you're focused on him. These minions are not particularly dangerous on their own but can overwhelm you if left unchecked. Use AoE attacks to deal with the minions quickly, and try to keep your focus on the Abyss King.

Phase 3: Final Stand of the Abyss King

When the Abyss King reaches a low health threshold, he will enter his final phase, which is a true test of your endurance and timing. His attacks become more erratic, and he gains access to powerful abilities that can deal devastating damage.

- **Phase Shift**: The Abyss King will teleport around the arena, reappearing in random locations. During this phase, keep your focus on him and anticipate where he will land. His attacks during teleportation are hard to dodge, so use your mobility to stay one step ahead of him.
- **Void Explosion**: As the final blow approaches, the Abyss King will start charging up for a devastating

Void Explosion. The explosion deals heavy damage and has a massive radius. You'll have a brief window of time before the explosion occurs, so quickly move to the farthest edge of the arena and prepare to dodge at the last second.

General Boss Fight Tips

- **Dodge with Precision**: The Abyss King's attacks have long wind-ups, allowing you to time your dodges precisely. Focus on dodging rather than blocking to preserve your stamina and energy for abilities and attacks.

- **Focus on Weaknesses**: Pay attention to when the Abyss King is most vulnerable. After certain attacks, such as the **Abyss Swipe** or **Ground Slam**, there are short windows of time where you can deal high damage. Use this time wisely to unload your strongest attacks.

- **Use Mobility to Avoid Traps**: The environment plays a huge role in the Abyss King fight. Use mobility tools like your glider or hoverboard to avoid environmental hazards and keep yourself positioned away from the Abyss King's most devastating moves.

Tips for Victory and Completing the Game

Defeating the Abyss King isn't just about surviving the battle—it's also about completing the game and leaving your mark in the world of *Hyper Light Breaker*. Here are some tips for victory and how to fully complete your journey:

1. Master the Boss Mechanics

Throughout your battle with the Abyss King, remember that this fight is about understanding his mechanics. Practice dodging, countering, and exploiting his vulnerabilities. The better you can anticipate his attacks and counter them, the more successful you'll be.

2. Focus on Resource Management

Manage your resources carefully during the final fight. Healing items, energy, and ammo should be used wisely to maximize your chances of survival. Don't waste resources on unnecessary healing or abilities—save them for the critical moments.

3. Reflect on Your Journey

After defeating the Abyss King, take a moment to reflect on your journey. Completing *Hyper Light Breaker* requires skill, patience, and adaptability. The sense of accomplishment after defeating the final boss is the reward for all your efforts, so enjoy the victory!

Chapter 7

Multiplayer Mode: Teamwork and Co-op Strategies

Multiplayer mode in *Hyper Light Breaker* transforms the game into a dynamic, cooperative experience. Whether you're facing off against fierce regional bosses, exploring the vast world of Overgrowth, or just tackling tough enemies, working together as a team can make all the difference. Co-op play allows you to combine your strengths, coordinate attacks, and share resources, making it easier to overcome even the most challenging encounters. This section will guide you through setting up multiplayer, provide co-op tips on roles and strategies for teams, and offer insights into working together to defeat the final challenge, the Abyss King.

Setting Up Multiplayer: How to Play with Friends

Getting started with multiplayer in *Hyper Light Breaker* is straightforward, but there are a few things you need to know to ensure that everything runs smoothly.

1. Joining a Multiplayer Session

Multiplayer in *Hyper Light Breaker* supports up to three players, meaning you can team up with two other players for a fully cooperative experience. Here's how to get started:

- **Accessing Multiplayer**: To enter multiplayer mode, simply navigate to the multiplayer section in the main menu. If you're the host, you can choose to start a new game and invite friends to join you. If you're joining a game, select the session you want to enter and connect. You can invite friends from your platform's friend list or share a session code for easy access.

- **Host and Client Roles**: The host of the game is the one who controls the main world and progression. The client players (those joining the host's session) will be able to progress in terms of combat and exploration but may not affect the main world's story progression. However, any loot, upgrades, and resources gained during the session will carry over to the client players' games.

- **Seamless Co-op Experience**: Once you've joined a game, the world will seamlessly adapt to accommodate all players. You'll fight together, explore side by side, and tackle the challenges of the Overgrowth as a team.

2. Network and Performance Considerations

To ensure a smooth co-op experience, make sure everyone in the session has a stable internet connection. Multiplayer games rely on synchronization, and a laggy connection can make the gameplay experience frustrating. Here are some tips for a smoother experience:

- **Low Latency Connection**: Players should have a stable internet connection with low latency to avoid issues like lag, rubberbanding, or connection drops. Ethernet connections are preferable, but Wi-Fi can work fine if the signal is strong.
- **In-Game Settings**: Ensure that all players adjust their in-game settings for optimal performance, especially in terms of graphics and frame rate. The game can get intense during boss fights, and smooth performance will make the experience more enjoyable.

3. Inviting Friends and Setting Permissions

Inviting friends into your game is a simple process. Once you've set up a multiplayer session, send an invitation to your friends through the game's invite system or via a session code. You can also adjust permissions to control who can enter your game, ensuring that you only play with friends or trusted players.

- **Private vs. Public Sessions**: Choose whether you want to play in a private session (invite-only) or a public one where anyone can join. For optimal control over your session, it's best to keep it private when coordinating with a specific team.

Co-op Tips: Best Roles and Strategies for Teams

In multiplayer, team composition and strategy are key. The synergy between players can make all the difference in how efficiently you tackle the challenges of *Hyper Light*

Breaker. The game encourages players to adopt specific roles that complement each other, ensuring that every team member contributes meaningfully to the battle.

1. Defining Roles in Multiplayer

Effective teamwork relies on each player filling a distinct role within the group. Here are some of the best roles for players to adopt in a co-op setting:

- **Tank (Sentinel)**: The tank's primary responsibility is to absorb damage and protect the team. The Sentinel is the best class for this role due to their high health, shield abilities, and crowd control tactics. Tanks should focus on keeping enemies' attention on themselves, allowing other players to deal damage without being interrupted. They should always position themselves between the boss and their teammates, drawing aggro and using abilities like **Shield Block** and **Taunt** to manage enemy focus.

- **DPS (Damage Dealers - Berserker and Marksman)**: Damage dealers are focused on dealing as much damage as possible. The Berserker and Marksman classes are ideal for this role, with the Berserker excelling in close combat and the Marksman excelling at long-range precision. As a DPS player, your goal is to exploit the boss's weaknesses during windows of vulnerability while avoiding getting hit yourself. Whether you're up close with a melee weapon or standing back and firing from a distance, your job is to inflict maximum damage quickly.

- **Support (Engineer)**: The Engineer class excels in providing support to the team. Whether through healing drones, defensive turrets, or EMP bursts, the Engineer plays a pivotal role in ensuring that the team stays alive and can handle tough enemies. As a support player, your role is to deploy healing drones when teammates are injured, use turrets to deal additional damage, and disrupt enemy attacks when possible. You'll also want to use defensive abilities to keep the tank alive and assist in controlling the battlefield.

2. Teamwork and Communication

Clear communication is essential in co-op play, especially during intense boss fights. To ensure your team is in sync and capable of handling whatever the game throws at you, here are some key strategies:

- **Callouts**: Always communicate with your teammates about the boss's movements, upcoming attacks, and where to focus fire. Let your team know when to fall back, when to focus on healing, or when to push forward for a finishing blow.

- **Ability Timing**: Coordinate the use of abilities between players. For instance, if the tank is about to use their **Taunt** ability, make sure the DPS players are ready to capitalize on the boss's vulnerability. If the Engineer is deploying a healing drone, make sure it's placed in a spot where everyone can benefit from it.

- **Role-Specific Tactics**: Always adhere to your assigned role. The tank should keep the enemy occupied, while the DPS focuses on dealing damage. The support should monitor the team's health and position, ensuring that everyone stays alive throughout the battle.

3. Positioning and Movement

Proper positioning is critical for success in boss fights, especially when there's a lot of movement and environmental hazards. Here's how you can position your team for maximum efficiency:

- **Tank Positioning**: The tank should always be at the front, in the boss's line of sight, ready to absorb damage. Make sure to position yourself between the boss and your DPS players, so they can focus on dealing damage without getting hit.

- **DPS Positioning**: DPS players should focus on staying behind the tank, either in melee range (if you're a Berserker) or at range (if you're a Marksman). Stay mobile and be aware of environmental hazards. In boss fights with large AoE attacks, make sure to move to a safe area when necessary and don't stay in the line of fire.

- **Support Positioning**: Support players, such as Engineers, should find positions where they can safely deploy drones and turrets, without getting too close to the enemy. Stay close enough to the tank to heal them if needed, but avoid drawing aggro.

- **Use the Arena**: Utilize the environment to your advantage. Many arenas have cover, high ground, or obstacles that can protect your team or provide a strategic advantage. Use these elements to create choke points or to avoid AoE damage from the boss.

Working Together to Defeat the Abyss King

The Abyss King represents the ultimate test of your team's coordination and skill. As a cooperative multiplayer fight, taking down the Abyss King requires a well-organized team that communicates, adapts, and works together to exploit the boss's weaknesses. Here's how to approach the final battle as a team:

1. Managing the Fight Phases

The Abyss King has multiple phases, each with its own set of mechanics and challenges. In multiplayer, your team will need to adapt quickly to each phase.

- **Phase 1 - Standard Attacks**: In the first phase, the Abyss King will use standard attacks, including swipes, fireballs, and his roar. The tank should focus on drawing aggro, while the DPS players deal damage. The support player should monitor everyone's health and deploy healing drones or shields as needed. Be prepared to dodge the Abyss

King's AoE attacks, especially his **Roar of the Abyss**, which can stun players.

- **Phase 2 - Enraged State**: When the Abyss King becomes enraged, his attacks become faster and more aggressive. The DPS players should continue their focus on damage, while the tank's role becomes more crucial—use the **Taunt** ability to keep the boss's attention. The support player should be ready to provide healing and deploy turrets to help manage the additional enemies or minions summoned by the Abyss King.

- **Phase 3 - Final Stand**: In the final phase, the Abyss King's attacks are faster, and his **Void Explosion** can wipe out players if they aren't positioned correctly. The tank should ensure they're drawing aggro, while the DPS players focus on dealing damage during moments when the Abyss King is vulnerable. The support player should keep everyone's health high, especially during the **Void Explosion**, which requires all players to be positioned in safe zones.

2. Staying Adaptive

In multiplayer, adaptability is key. The Abyss King has several phases, and each one requires a shift in strategy. If your current tactics aren't working, don't be afraid to adjust. Have the support player switch to more aggressive healing or buffing abilities, and have DPS players experiment with different weapons to maximize damage.

Communication is essential to making these adjustments quickly and effectively. Make sure everyone knows when to change roles, reposition, or prepare for a specific attack phase.

Chapter 8

Exploring the Hub City in *Hyper Light Breaker*

The Hub City in *Hyper Light Breaker* is your sanctuary between runs—a place where you can regroup, upgrade your character, and prepare for your next venture into the perilous Overgrowth. Unlike the brutal and unpredictable world of the Overgrowth, the Hub City offers a calm and strategic environment where you can reflect on your progress, interact with NPCs, and unlock crucial upgrades and resources. This section will guide you through what you can do in the Hub City, how to engage with NPCs and understand the comic book-style storytelling, and where to find shops, upgrades, and secrets to improve your chances in the next run.

What You Can Do in the Hub Between Runs

The Hub City acts as your central point of respite and preparation. After each run, whether successful or not, you'll return to the Hub to catch your breath, enhance your Breaker, and plan your next steps. Here's a breakdown of the essential activities you can do in the Hub City:

1. Replenish Your Resources

After each run, your resources—health, energy, and ammo—are often depleted, and it's crucial to restock before heading back into the Overgrowth. The Hub City offers several ways to replenish your supplies:

- **Health Recovery**: You'll find stations or NPCs in the Hub that offer healing services, where you can recover health or purchase health-restoring items. Managing your health pool between runs is essential, so be sure to top off your health before embarking on another dangerous adventure.

- **Energy Recharges**: Similar to health, your energy is consumed by the use of abilities. Energy stations are available in the Hub to restore your ability to use special powers, or you can purchase energy-refilling items that you can take with you on your next run.

- **Ammo and Consumables**: You can purchase ammo for your ranged weapons, as well as consumables like grenades, traps, or other useful items that help during your exploration of the Overgrowth. These can be bought from various vendors located around the Hub.

2. Customize and Upgrade Your Breaker

The Hub City is your primary location for upgrading your Breaker's equipment, abilities, and skills. Between runs, you'll have access to a variety of customization options that will directly influence your performance in the Overgrowth.

- **Weapon Upgrades**: Visit the blacksmith or weapon specialist to upgrade your weapons, making them more powerful, durable, or versatile. You can enhance your weapons with new stats, added elemental effects, or specialized damage boosts that will give you an edge in combat.

- **Ability Enhancements**: You'll also be able to upgrade your abilities to make them more effective. Depending on your class, you can choose to increase the potency of your attacks, extend the duration of shields, or decrease the cooldown time between ability uses. These upgrades are vital for improving your combat efficiency.

- **Armor and Equipment**: Upgrading your armor and equipment is key to surviving tougher encounters. In the Hub, you can visit armorers to enhance your defensive gear. This includes upgrading your armor's durability, resistance to specific damage types (fire, electric, etc.), and adding new passive effects like increased stamina or regeneration.

3. Check for New Missions and Side Quests

While the main objective is to defeat the regional bosses and ultimately the Abyss King, the Hub City is also where you can find additional missions and side quests that help strengthen your Breaker. These quests often reward you with valuable items, new equipment, or lore that enriches the game world.

- **Side Quests**: These smaller, optional tasks can provide unique rewards that improve your overall build. They may involve hunting down rare resources, defeating mini-bosses, or rescuing NPCs in trouble. Completing these quests helps you gather additional items and experience that can give you the edge in your journey through the Overgrowth.

- **Bounty Hunts**: Some NPCs in the Hub may offer bounties to hunt down specific enemies or bosses that have terrorized nearby regions. These bounties reward you with significant loot, including rare items, crafting materials, and upgrade tokens.

4. Socialize and Build Relationships with NPCs

The NPCs in the Hub City offer more than just services—they are integral to the game's lore and progression. Engaging with NPCs will reveal more about the world, provide valuable information, and unlock additional features.

- **Dialogues and Lore**: Some NPCs will offer brief, interactive dialogue through the comic book panels. These interactions allow you to learn more about the history of the Overgrowth, the Abyss King, and other significant events that shape the game's world. While there are no spoken dialogues, the visual storytelling through these comic panels adds depth and immersion to the experience.

- **Unlocking Secrets**: Interacting with specific NPCs may also unlock hidden secrets, new gameplay mechanics, or even new locations for you to explore. Keep an eye on the characters you meet—they may have valuable information or offer upgrades that you can't find elsewhere.

NPC Interactions: Understanding Comic Book Panels and Storytelling

Hyper Light Breaker employs a unique method of storytelling through comic book-style panels, allowing players to engage with the narrative visually rather than through spoken dialogue. This method not only enhances the game's aesthetic but also deepens the immersive experience. Here's how you can understand and interact with the game's comic book storytelling:

1. Visual Storytelling Through Panels

When interacting with NPCs in the Hub City or encountering important story moments, you'll see comic book panels that depict key dialogue, events, and lore. These panels don't contain any voiceover but rely on visuals, animations, and text to convey the plot.

- **Character and Event Panels**: When an NPC speaks or when a significant event unfolds, the screen transitions to a panel featuring the character(s) involved. The text will typically describe the situation or the character's thoughts, often accompanied by visual cues that suggest emotions or tone. Pay attention to the background, character expressions, and colors, as they often hint at the deeper meanings or emotions behind the scene.

- **Non-Verbal Communication**: Some NPCs may only communicate through actions or visual cues. For example, an NPC might gesture or use body language to convey their intentions or feelings, providing you with subtle hints about their personality or the world around you.

- **Lore and Worldbuilding**: Comic book panels often reveal significant lore about the Overgrowth, its inhabitants, and its history. These narrative elements are crucial for understanding the bigger picture and will provide valuable insights into the game's deeper mysteries. Keep an eye on recurring visual motifs or symbols that may indicate important plot points.

2. Using Comic Panels for Strategic Insights

While the comic panels primarily serve to tell the story, they also provide useful strategic insights:

- **Boss and Enemy Information**: Some NPCs will provide hints or detailed information about upcoming bosses or enemies. This may be in the form of a comic book panel showing the enemy's weaknesses or telling you about past battles. Use this information to prepare for tough fights in the Overgrowth.

- **Mission Objectives**: When accepting missions or side quests, the comic panels can show you important details, such as objectives, rewards, and key locations. These panels ensure that you always know where to go and what to do next, without the need for lengthy text-heavy dialogue.

Shops, Upgrades, and Secrets to Unlock in the Hub

The Hub City is not just a place to rest and heal; it's also filled with shops, upgrades, and hidden secrets that can significantly enhance your journey through *Hyper Light Breaker*. Here's a guide to maximizing what the Hub City has to offer:

1. Shops and Vendors

The Hub contains various shops where you can purchase essential items, upgrades, and resources for your next run. These shops are run by NPCs who provide you with essential tools to improve your Breaker's abilities.

- **Weapon and Armor Shops**: Here, you can purchase or upgrade your weapons and armor. These shops offer everything from basic gear to rare, powerful items. They also sell unique enhancements, such as elemental modifications for your weapons or defensive upgrades for your armor.

- **Consumables and Resources**: Stock up on consumables like healing potions, ammo, energy boosters, and buffs. Some items are rare and can only be found in these shops, so be sure to check in between runs to ensure you're fully prepared for the challenges ahead.

2. Upgrade Stations

Upgrade stations are scattered throughout the Hub and allow you to enhance your Breaker's abilities and gear. These stations typically require special resources or currency to use, which you'll acquire by completing missions or exploring the Overgrowth.

- **Ability Enhancements**: These stations allow you to upgrade your abilities, increasing their effectiveness or reducing cooldowns. You can improve offensive abilities, like increasing damage, or defensive ones, like extending shield duration or reducing energy costs.

- **Weapon Modifications**: If you have the necessary resources, you can upgrade your weapons with additional effects, such as elemental damage, increased attack speed, or improved durability. These modifications are critical for tackling tougher enemies and bosses in the Overgrowth.

3. Secrets to Unlock

The Hub City is full of secrets, hidden areas, and Easter eggs waiting to be discovered. These secrets often require you to complete certain objectives, interact with specific NPCs, or explore obscure parts of the Hub.

- **Hidden Lore**: Some secrets include hidden lore about the world, its history, and the Abyss King. Unlocking these pieces of information provides a deeper understanding of the game's narrative and gives you clues about what to expect next.

- **Special Items**: You may stumble upon rare items, unique weapons, or powerful upgrades that are only available through exploration or special interactions with NPCs. Keep exploring the Hub and interacting with its inhabitants to uncover everything it has to offer.

- **Alternate Paths and Locations**: There may be hidden paths within the Hub City that lead to special areas, shops, or NPCs. These can offer rare rewards, such as exclusive abilities or gear. Make sure to explore every corner to find these hidden gems.

Chapter 9

Secrets, Easter Eggs, and Unlockables in *Hyper Light Breaker*

Hyper Light Breaker is packed with hidden features, Easter eggs, and unlockable content that add depth and excitement to the game. Whether you're an avid explorer looking for secrets or a completionist striving to find every collectible, there's a wealth of hidden treasures awaiting you. These secrets not only enhance the overall experience but also reward you with valuable items, lore, and even new gameplay mechanics. In this section, we'll dive into how to uncover these hidden features, unlock Easter eggs, and find all the collectibles scattered throughout the world of Overgrowth.

Hidden Features and Special Secrets

One of the joys of *Hyper Light Breaker* lies in its ability to surprise players with hidden features that aren't immediately obvious. These secrets are often tucked away in corners of the world that require keen observation, clever thinking, or a bit of extra effort to discover. Here are some key hidden features and secrets you can look out for:

1. Hidden Lore and Story Elements

As you explore the Overgrowth, you'll uncover hidden lore that provides a deeper understanding of the world, its history, and the forces at play. These pieces of lore can be discovered in various ways, such as through environmental storytelling, secret NPC interactions, or uncovering ancient ruins.

- **Environmental Storytelling**: Look for cryptic messages, ancient murals, or ruins that tell the story of past civilizations. These can provide valuable clues about the lore of the Abyss King and other significant events that shape the Overgrowth.

- **Secret NPCs**: Some NPCs will only appear in hidden areas or after completing certain objectives. Interacting with these characters may unlock new quests, provide additional lore, or offer upgrades and rewards.

2. Secret Areas and Hidden Paths

The Overgrowth is a sprawling, interconnected world, and there are many secret areas and hidden paths that you may not encounter during your usual run. These areas often require keen exploration, including climbing, using special movement mechanics, or finding hidden levers and switches.

- **Climbing and Wall Running**: Use your climbing skills to scale walls, reach higher platforms, or navigate through narrow gaps that might lead to hidden rooms or valuable loot.

- **Invisible Paths**: In certain areas, paths may appear invisible or hidden from plain sight. These paths can be unlocked by interacting with specific objects in the environment or completing certain conditions. Watch for subtle environmental cues that hint at these secret paths.

- **Hidden Ruins or Dungeons**: Keep an eye out for hidden ruins or dungeons that aren't immediately accessible. These areas often house powerful enemies, valuable loot, and lore. To access these secret dungeons, you may need to solve environmental puzzles, defeat hidden minibosses, or complete specific quests.

3. Rare Artifacts and Collectibles

Throughout the game, you'll come across rare artifacts, collectibles, and special items that can only be found by exploring off the beaten path. These collectibles often unlock new gameplay elements, provide powerful upgrades, or enhance the story.

- **Ancient Artifacts**: Scattered throughout the Overgrowth are ancient artifacts that offer bonuses to your character. These artifacts could boost your health, energy, or give you access to new abilities. Some of these items can only be found by completing specific objectives or finding hidden locations in the world.

- **Hidden Vaults**: In certain regions of the Overgrowth, hidden vaults can be unlocked by solving complex puzzles or defeating difficult enemies. These vaults contain high-level loot, including exclusive weapons, armor, and unique abilities. Finding and unlocking these vaults requires patience and keen observation of your surroundings.

How to Unlock Easter Eggs and Bonus Content

Easter eggs and bonus content are scattered throughout *Hyper Light Breaker*, providing fun and rewarding surprises for players who go beyond the main objectives. These Easter eggs often reference the game's developers, the *Hyper Light* series, or other elements of gaming culture. Here's how to find and unlock these hidden gems:

1. Developer Easter Eggs and References

Hyper Light Breaker includes a number of references to its own development and to other popular games. These Easter eggs are often hidden in the game world or tied to specific actions.

- **Developer Rooms**: In some areas, you may find hidden rooms or secret passages that are filled with nods to the game's development team. These rooms may contain hidden messages or other Easter eggs that pay homage to the team behind the game.

- **Classic Game References**: Keep an eye out for objects, symbols, or NPCs that reference other games in the *Hyper Light* series or popular games in general. These references are often subtle, but they add an extra layer of depth and humor to the game.

2. Unlockable Bonus Content

As you progress through the game, you may unlock special bonus content that enhances the experience or offers additional challenges.

- **Alternate Skins and Cosmetics**: By completing certain challenges or finding hidden items, you can unlock alternate skins for your Breaker or cosmetic items that allow you to customize your character. These skins often provide a fresh look and allow you to personalize your gameplay experience.

- **New Abilities or Weapons**: Some Easter eggs unlock new abilities, weapons, or special moves that give you an edge in combat. These can be found in hidden areas or by completing specific challenges. They may not be immediately essential to progressing in the game, but they add new layers of gameplay for those who seek to explore everything the game has to offer.

3. Hidden Dialogues and Alternate Endings

Another fun Easter egg to uncover in *Hyper Light Breaker* is the possibility of alternate endings. By making specific choices or completing certain tasks, you may unlock hidden dialogues or even alternative endings that provide a deeper understanding of the world and the Abyss King.

- **Secret Interactions**: Some NPCs in the Hub City will offer additional dialogue options based on your choices or progress. These secret interactions can unlock hidden lore or offer alternative perspectives on the story.

- **Multiple Endings**: Depending on the choices you make during the game, you may encounter different endings. Some of these endings require specific conditions to be met, such as completing a set of secret side quests or unlocking hidden abilities.

Tips for Finding All the Collectibles

If you're aiming to find every collectible, Easter egg, and secret in *Hyper Light Breaker*, it's important to stay methodical and observant. Here are some tips to help you uncover every hidden feature:

1. Explore Every Corner

The key to finding collectibles is exploration. Don't rush through areas—take your time to explore every nook and cranny. Look behind walls, check for hidden paths, and climb to high vantage points to scan for collectibles or hidden items.

- **Use Your Abilities**: Don't forget to utilize all of your movement abilities, like climbing and gliding, to reach high or hidden areas. Some collectibles may only be accessible through clever use of these mechanics.
- **Environmental Clues**: The game often provides subtle environmental clues that hint at hidden areas or secrets. Pay attention to unusual markings on the

ground, hidden switches, or gaps in walls that may lead to off-the-beaten-path locations.

2. Track Your Progress

As you explore the Overgrowth, take note of areas you haven't fully explored. Certain collectibles or Easter eggs are locked behind specific conditions or hidden in areas that are only accessible after you've progressed in the game or completed side quests.

- **Use the Map**: The game's map can help you keep track of areas that you've explored. If you've missed something, the map will often highlight unexplored locations or regions where secrets might be hidden.

- **Collectible Checklist**: Some players prefer to keep a checklist of all the collectibles they've found, including lore pieces, hidden artifacts, and Easter eggs. This ensures that you don't miss anything important and helps you stay on track.

3. Keep an Eye on NPCs

Many NPCs in the Hub City provide valuable information or hint at hidden secrets. Some will offer side quests that lead to rare collectibles, while others may unlock special dialogues or lore if you engage with them enough.

- **Complete Side Quests**: Completing side quests can often lead to new areas or collectible rewards. Don't skip these quests, as they frequently unlock hidden items or lore pieces.

4. Stay Curious

Finally, the most important tip is to stay curious. *Hyper Light Breaker* is filled with secrets, and often the most rewarding discoveries are made when you least expect them. Push the boundaries of exploration and don't hesitate to revisit previously explored areas, as they may change or reveal new secrets as the game progresses.

Chapter 10

Advanced Tips for Mastering

Hyper Light Breaker

Hyper Light Breaker is a game that challenges players to master its intricate combat mechanics, strategic use of abilities, and effective resource management. Whether you're facing off against regional bosses or navigating the ever-changing Overgrowth, the more advanced your gameplay techniques, the better prepared you'll be for the game's toughest challenges. This section will cover advanced combat techniques, tips for optimizing your abilities and gear, and strategies for managing your runs effectively. With these tips in hand, you'll be able to enhance your gameplay, maximize efficiency, and truly master *Hyper Light Breaker*.

Advanced Combat Techniques and Tricks

Mastering combat in *Hyper Light Breaker* is about more than just button-mashing—it's about precision, timing, and adapting your strategies on the fly. Here are some advanced combat techniques that will elevate your performance:

1. Mastering the Dodge and Counter System

Dodge mechanics are crucial for surviving in *Hyper Light Breaker*. Dodging isn't just about avoiding damage—it's about positioning yourself for a counterattack. Here's how you can take dodging to the next level:

- **Perfect Dodge**: A perfect dodge, timed right before an enemy's attack lands, grants you an invulnerability frame and a short window of time to counterattack. This can be the difference between dodging a deadly blow and turning the tide of a fight.

- **Dodge and Follow Up**: After dodging an enemy's attack, immediately follow up with a combo of your own. By mastering the timing between dodges and attacks, you can build powerful attack chains without leaving yourself vulnerable. Practice timing your melee combos or ranged shots right after a dodge to keep the pressure on your enemies.

- **Dodge Directionally**: Instead of dodging randomly, try to dodge toward the enemy's weak spots. For example, dodge to the side of an incoming attack and position yourself behind the enemy for a rear strike. This technique is particularly useful when fighting bosses with large AoE attacks, as you can evade and reposition for the next strike.

2. Fluid Melee and Ranged Combos

While you may prefer one combat style, *Hyper Light Breaker* rewards players who fluidly switch between melee and ranged combat. Here's how you can maximize the effectiveness of both:

- **Melee to Ranged Switch**: In combat, seamlessly switch between melee and ranged attacks for maximum efficiency. For example, use a sword for quick melee combos and then immediately switch to a bow for long-range precision shots. This not only keeps the enemies guessing but also allows you to stay mobile and adaptable.

- **Close Combat with Ranged Back-Up**: When you're surrounded by enemies, start with close-range combat to clear out smaller enemies. Then, switch to a ranged weapon to target the tougher foes from a safe distance. This combination allows you to efficiently deal with crowds while also picking off high-priority targets.

- **Exploit Enemy Weaknesses**: Each enemy has its own weaknesses, whether it's vulnerability to elemental damage, specific weak spots, or vulnerabilities after a certain attack. Use your melee abilities to provoke these weaknesses and quickly transition to your ranged weapons for finishing blows. Knowing when to exploit these moments will maximize your damage output.

3. Utilizing Elemental Damage and Abilities

Elemental damage adds an extra layer of depth to combat. You can tailor your abilities and weapon choices based on the enemies you're facing.

- **Elemental Weaknesses**: Many enemies are weak to specific elemental damage types, such as fire, ice, or lightning. Equip weapons or abilities that exploit these weaknesses. For instance, if you're facing a mechanical boss, use electrical-based attacks to short-circuit its systems. Conversely, use fire-based attacks against enemies vulnerable to heat or burn effects.

- **Elemental Combos**: Some abilities and weapons allow you to combine elements for devastating effects. For example, you can use a fire ability to ignite an enemy and then switch to an ice attack to freeze it, immobilizing the target for a critical follow-up strike. Experiment with different elements to discover powerful combos that suit your playstyle.

4. Managing Stamina and Resources in Combat

While you may be focused on attacking, it's equally important to manage your stamina, energy, and health during combat. Here's how to efficiently balance your resources:

- **Stamina Management**: Every melee attack and dodge consumes stamina. Running out of stamina mid-fight can leave you vulnerable, so pay attention to your stamina bar. Use defensive abilities when your stamina is low and wait for it to regenerate before diving back into aggressive combat.

- **Energy Management**: Your abilities require energy to activate. Keep track of your energy bar and avoid wasting it on low-priority attacks. Conserve energy for when you need it most, such as during boss fights or when faced with multiple enemies at once.

How to Optimize Abilities and Gear for Maximum Efficiency

To truly master *Hyper Light Breaker*, you need to understand how to optimize your Breaker's abilities and gear for maximum efficiency. The right combination of upgrades, gear, and abilities can make all the difference in combat.

1. Tailoring Your Build to Your Playstyle

Customization is key when it comes to optimizing your Breaker. Choose gear and abilities that align with how you want to play. Here's how to create the perfect build for your preferred playstyle:

- **Aggressive Melee Build (Berserker)**: If you prefer close combat, focus on upgrading abilities that enhance your attack speed, damage, and survivability. Upgrade abilities like **Rage Unleashed** to boost your offensive capabilities and **Iron Will** to reduce damage taken. Pair these abilities with melee weapons that deal heavy damage and invest in armor that increases health.

- **Precision Ranged Build (Marksman)**: For ranged combat, focus on abilities that enhance your mobility and damage output. Abilities like **Precision Shot** and **Explosive Arrow** should be upgraded to maximize your ranged damage. Equip armor that boosts stamina and energy regeneration, ensuring that you have enough resources to stay mobile and deal consistent damage from a distance.

- **Balanced Support Build (Engineer)**: Engineers should focus on enhancing their ability to support teammates while also dealing damage. Upgrade abilities like **Healing Drones** to provide consistent healing, and **Turret Deployment** to create extra firepower. Equip gear that improves your ability to generate energy and enhance your gadgets, allowing you to provide buffs and control the battlefield.

2. Prioritizing Weapon and Ability Synergy

Your gear and abilities should complement each other for the best results. For example, if you're playing as a Berserker, focus on upgrading abilities that increase your damage output and sustain. Pair this with heavy-hitting melee weapons like axes or polearms that match your aggressive style. Similarly, if you're a Marksman, invest in abilities that enhance your precision and range, and equip weapons that provide utility and high damage, such as crossbows or bows.

- **Weapon Affinity**: Make sure your weapon matches the abilities you're upgrading. For example, if you're boosting melee abilities, you'll want a weapon that provides fast, heavy damage with the potential for combos. If you're focusing on ranged attacks, equip weapons that enhance your ability to hit targets from a distance and unlock abilities that reduce cooldown times for quick successive shots.

3. Gear Upgrades for Max Efficiency

As you progress through the game, upgrading your gear becomes essential. Focus on upgrading armor and weapons that provide a balance of offense and defense. Here's how to prioritize your upgrades:

- **Weapon Upgrades**: Always prioritize upgrading your weapons for maximum damage. Look for opportunities to add elemental effects or special bonuses to your weapons. This increases your overall damage output and gives you an edge against enemies with elemental weaknesses.

- **Armor Upgrades**: Your armor should offer both defensive capabilities and buffs that suit your playstyle. Focus on upgrading armor that increases health, stamina, and energy regeneration, as these will allow you to fight longer and recover faster during intense battles. For tank builds like the Sentinel, focus on armor that boosts resistance to damage types, such as fire or ice.

Managing Runs: Resource Gathering, Upgrades, and More

Efficiently managing your runs is critical for ensuring you're prepared for the challenges ahead. Here's how you can make the most of your time in the Overgrowth and optimize your resource gathering, upgrades, and general progression:

1. Resource Gathering Efficiency

Resource management is a key component of surviving in *Hyper Light Breaker*. As you venture into the Overgrowth, focus on gathering the necessary resources to sustain yourself.

- **Prioritize Key Resources**: Always keep an eye out for resources that are essential to your survival, such as healing items, energy boosters, and crafting materials. These can often be found in hidden areas or after defeating powerful enemies.

- **Loot Management**: Collect loot from defeated enemies and search every corner of the Overgrowth for hidden chests or containers. Make sure to regularly return to the Hub to check in with vendors for upgrades and stock up on resources.

2. Upgrades Between Runs

The Hub City is where you'll be able to use the resources you've gathered to upgrade your Breaker and equipment. Here's how to use your resources most efficiently:

- **Upgrading Weapons First**: Prioritize weapon upgrades early in the game to improve your damage output. This is particularly important if you're struggling with tougher enemies or bosses. Upgrading your gear ensures that you're always prepared for the challenges ahead.

- **Ability Enhancements**: Don't forget to upgrade your abilities, as this will significantly impact your performance. Focus on enhancing core abilities that suit your playstyle, such as damage buffs or mobility-enhancing abilities.

3. Balancing Risk and Reward

As you explore the Overgrowth, the game presents you with tough decisions. Should you push forward to explore more dangerous areas for greater rewards, or should you return to the Hub to upgrade and prepare for the next run? The key is to find a balance between risk and reward.

- **Risk Management**: As you progress, consider the difficulty of the areas you're entering. If you're low on resources or health, it may be wise to return to the Hub for a restock and upgrade before venturing into more dangerous territory.

- **Strategic Exploration**: Focus your exploration on areas that offer high reward, such as hidden vaults or minibosses that drop valuable loot. The more you explore, the better equipped you'll

Chapter 11

Troubleshooting and Frequently Asked Questions

No game is without its challenges, and *Hyper Light Breaker* is no exception. Whether you're a seasoned player or just starting your journey through the Overgrowth, you may encounter technical issues or have questions about gameplay mechanics. In this section, we'll address common problems players may face, answer frequently asked questions, and offer performance and technical tips to ensure you have the best possible experience in *Hyper Light Breaker*.

Solving Common Issues in Hyper Light Breaker

While *Hyper Light Breaker* is a well-polished game, certain issues can arise. Here are some common problems players encounter, along with solutions to resolve them:

1. Crashes or Freezes During Gameplay

If the game crashes or freezes during gameplay, it can be frustrating, especially during intense boss battles or exploration.

- **Solution:**

- **Check System Requirements**: Ensure your PC or console meets the minimum system requirements for *Hyper Light Breaker*. Insufficient hardware can lead to crashes or freezes.

- **Update Drivers**: Make sure your graphics card and other important drivers are up-to-date. Outdated drivers can cause performance issues and crashes.

- **Lower Graphics Settings**: If you experience frequent crashes, try lowering the graphics settings in the game's options menu to reduce the strain on your system.

- **Verify Game Files**: If you're playing on PC, try verifying the integrity of the game files through the game client (Steam, Epic Games, etc.) to ensure that no files are missing or corrupted.

- **Close Background Applications**: Close any unnecessary applications running in the background to free up system resources and prevent crashes.

2. Multiplayer Connection Issues

Multiplayer connectivity problems are common in online games, especially when trying to join a session with friends.

- **Solution**:

- **Check Internet Connection**: Ensure all players have a stable and fast internet connection. Lag, disconnects, or delays can be caused by poor internet performance.
- **Host Session Stability**: If you are the host, make sure your internet connection is stable. The host's connection is crucial for smooth multiplayer sessions.
- **Restart the Game**: Sometimes, simply restarting the game or your platform can resolve connection issues. If you're having trouble joining a session, try restarting the game or logging out and back into your account.
- **Session Code and Invite**: If you're having trouble joining a friend's session, double-check the session code or ensure you've received an invite. Sometimes, errors can occur with session invitations or codes.

3. Input Lag or Delayed Controls

Input lag can significantly affect gameplay, especially during fast-paced combat sections.

- **Solution**:
  - **Check Controller Connection**: If you're using a controller, make sure it is properly connected to your system. Wireless controllers, in particular, can sometimes have lag due to interference or low battery.

- **Reduce Graphical Load**: Input lag can be exacerbated by high graphical settings. Lower the settings in the game's menu to reduce graphical strain on your system, which can help with responsiveness.
- **Use a Wired Connection**: For those experiencing input lag with wireless controllers, consider switching to a wired connection to reduce lag.

4. Game Not Launching

If *Hyper Light Breaker* fails to launch or starts up with an error message, there are a few things you can try.

- **Solution**:
    - **Reboot the System**: Restart your PC or console to clear any potential conflicts or issues.
    - **Check for Updates**: Make sure that the game, your system, and any necessary software (like drivers or game platforms) are fully updated.
    - **Check for Antivirus Interference**: Sometimes, antivirus software can block certain game files from launching. Temporarily disable your antivirus and try launching the game again.
    - **Reinstall the Game**: If none of the above works, uninstall the game and reinstall it.

This can often fix issues caused by corrupted game files.

Frequently Asked Questions by New and Experienced Players

1. How Do I Change My Breaker Class?

In *Hyper Light Breaker*, your class determines your abilities and combat style. However, you cannot directly change your class mid-run. To switch classes, you will need to start a new run from the Hub and select a different class before venturing into the Overgrowth.

- **Tip**: Experiment with different classes to find the one that suits your preferred playstyle. Each class has its own strengths and weaknesses, so feel free to try them all.

2. Can I Play *Hyper Light Breaker* Solo?

Yes, *Hyper Light Breaker* can be played solo, and it offers a rewarding experience for single-player gameplay. You'll face the same challenges as in multiplayer, but with the added advantage of controlling the entire team yourself (if you wish). The game dynamically scales with the number of players, so solo play may be slightly more challenging, but it's fully doable with proper preparation.

- **Tip**: If you're playing solo, consider using the Sentinel class for tanking or the Engineer for support. These classes provide a good balance of offense and defense and can help you survive longer in solo runs.

3. How Can I Unlock New Weapons or Abilities?

Weapons and abilities are unlocked as you progress through the game. Completing side quests, defeating regional bosses, or finding hidden areas will reward you with new weapons, upgrades, and abilities.

- **Tip**: Keep exploring every nook and cranny of the Overgrowth and complete side quests to unlock the best gear. Rare weapons and abilities are often hidden in secret locations, so be thorough in your exploration.

4. Are There Multiple Endings in *Hyper Light Breaker*?

Yes, *Hyper Light Breaker* offers multiple endings based on your choices throughout the game, particularly in how you engage with certain NPCs or complete specific side quests.

- **Tip**: If you're aiming for a specific ending, be sure to keep track of your choices and any major decisions made throughout the game. Different paths can lead to different outcomes, so experimenting with these choices can provide a fresh perspective on the story.

5. Can I Play *Hyper Light Breaker* Without Multiplayer?

Yes, *Hyper Light Breaker* is designed to be enjoyed both solo and in multiplayer. While the multiplayer mode adds a fun cooperative element, the single-player experience is rich enough to enjoy on its own. You won't miss out on any core gameplay features by playing solo.

Performance and Technical Tips for a Smooth Experience

To ensure that *Hyper Light Breaker* runs smoothly on your system, follow these performance and technical tips:

1. Adjust Graphics Settings

If you're experiencing lag or poor performance, reducing the graphical settings can help improve your experience, especially if you're playing on lower-end hardware.

- **Resolution**: Lower the resolution to improve performance if your system is struggling to maintain a high frame rate. A slight drop in resolution can have a significant impact on game performance without sacrificing too much visual quality.

- **Graphics Quality**: Reduce settings like shadows, textures, and ambient occlusion to lower levels. These settings can be adjusted for a smoother experience without compromising core gameplay mechanics.

2. Keep Your System Updated

Ensure that your operating system, graphics drivers, and the game itself are all up-to-date. Developers frequently release patches to address bugs and performance issues, so keeping everything current is essential for a smooth experience.

- **Check for Game Patches**: Occasionally, *Hyper Light Breaker* may receive patches that address performance or bug-related issues. Check for updates regularly to ensure you're playing the most optimized version of the game.

3. Disable Background Processes

Running too many applications in the background can drain system resources, resulting in lower performance. Close unnecessary apps and processes to free up CPU and memory for the game.

- **Task Manager (PC)**: Use the task manager (Ctrl + Shift + Esc) to check which processes are using up resources and close them before starting the game.

4. Use a Wired Connection (Multiplayer)

For the best multiplayer experience, always use a wired connection if possible. A stable Ethernet connection will reduce the likelihood of lag or disconnections, ensuring that your co-op sessions run smoothly.

5. Reinstall the Game

If you're facing ongoing issues that can't be resolved through simple troubleshooting, consider reinstalling the game. This can fix corrupted files, improve performance, and provide a fresh start if you've encountered persistent problems.

www.ingramcontent.com/pod-product-compliance
Lightning Source LLC
Chambersburg PA
CBHW070151230526
45471CB00002B/614